JEREMY P. TARCHER/PENGUIN
Published by the Penguin Group
Penguin Group (USA) Inc., 375 Hudson Street, New York, New York 10014, USA •
Penguin Group (Canada), 90 Eglinton Avenue East, Suite 700, Toronto, Ontario M4P
2Y3, Canada (a division of Pearson Penguin Canada Inc.) • Penguin Books Ltd, 80
Strand, London WC2R 0RL, England • Penguin Ireland, 25 St Stephen's Green,
Dublin 2, Ireland (a division of Penguin Books Ltd) • Penguin Group (Australia), 250
Camberwell Road, Camberwell, Victoria 3124, Australia (a division of Pearson Australia
Group Pty Ltd) • Penguin Books India Pvt Ltd, 11 Community Centre, Panchsheel
Park, New Delhi–110 017, India • Penguin Group (NZ), Cnr Airborne and Rosedale
Roads, Albany, Auckland 1310, New Zealand (a division of Pearson New Zealand Ltd)
• Penguin Books (South Africa) (Pty) Ltd, 24 Sturdee Avenue, Rosebank,
Johannesburg 2196, South Africa
Penguin Books Ltd, Registered Offices:
80 Strand, London WC2R 0RL, England

Most Tarcher/Penguin books are available at special quantity discounts for bulk purchase
for sales promotions, premiums, fundraising, and educational needs. Special books or
book excerpts also can be created to fit specific needs. For details, write Penguin Group
(USA) Inc. Special Markets, 375 Hudson Street, New York, NY 10014.

Library of Congress Cataloging-in-Publication Data
Aschenbrand, Periel.
The only bush I trust is my own / Periel Aschenbrand.
p.   cm.
ISBN 1-58542-420-X
1. Sex—Humor.   2. Sex customs—United States—Humor.
3. Political satire, American.   I. Title.
PN6231.S54A83   2005
814'.6—dc22   2005041820

Printed in the United States of America
1   3   5   7   9   10   8   6   4   2

Book design by Stephanie Huntwork

the only bush
i trust is my own

the only bush
i trust is my own

periel aschenbrand

jeremy p. tarcher/penguin

a member of penguin group (usa) inc.

new york

In memory of Chana Wirnik and Monique Wittig, both of whom taught me a good deal about what it means to be *brave*.

And, of course, for my parents, without whom I would truly be nothing. I adore and appreciate both of you more than I could ever express.

If the readers do not feel the shock of words, then your work is not done.

—Monique Wittig

The only reason I'm in fashion is to destroy the word "conformity."

—Vivienne Westwood

acknowledgments

Ken Siman. For your vision, your unbelievable dedication, and for being mad enough to understand.

Eli S. Evans. For whom there are no words, and what can I offer except them?

Kathryn Phyllis Kimball. For showing me there *is* something worth believing in—you.

Kevin Greer. For your patience and your wonderful love. Without you, I would be a much smaller person.

Doug Stewart. For loving the work before you loved me, and for working so long to make this happen.

Mari Fujita. For letting me and teaching me and actually being everything I thought you were. And more.

Mark Seliger. For helping me realize my vision. I am one fortunate cookie to be so blessed to have found you.

Lissy Lu. Without you, many of the things I have done would not have been possible. You really are an angel.

Amanda Friedman. For your unwavering support and constant encouragement, and for sharing with me your wonderful art.

Erica Samuels and my "Round Table" girls. For being a bunch of true knockouts. Thank you all so much for working your asses off.

And to all the rest of you, and you know who you are, who have shared your stories with me and allowed me to write about you—particularly Erica, Doda Sara, and Nadir—I thank you, from the bottom of my heart.

contents

part one

word of wisdom

i'm on the phone with my mother and she's like, I'm very upset you're waitressing. It's terrible that someone with a master's degree is waitressing. You aren't using your God-given talents. Why not be a lawyer? In her Israeli accent she tells me, even if you never use it, a law degree is something you can always fall back on. You're a very good debater and you've always cared about the underdog. I think you would make a wonderful lawyer.

Me: I still remember when you not only wanted me to *be* a lawyer, but you also wanted me to *marry* a lawyer—a *Jewish* lawyer.

My mother: I don't know that it was necessarily a lawyer, but I did want you to marry someone Jewish. The Jewish people went through so much to keep our faith that it's very important, especially for when you have children.

Me: This is, of course, assuming that I have any interest in getting married and having children. Besides, I like being a waitress.

My mother: Well, that's unfortunate. And the way you dress—it's grungy-looking. I like people to look well groomed, and you have this gorgeous hair and instead of wearing it nicely, you just bunch it up, and it looks like god knows what, it looks like a nest. And it's a shame, it's really a shame. You have almost perfect hair.

Me: Why only almost?

My mother: Well, you have that wave in the back that I don't like. It would be perfect if you blew your hair dry, but you don't. It could be bouncy and shiny. And that black nail polish.

I was like, what's wrong with black nail polish?

My mother goes, I don't like the gothic look.

I'm like, Mommy, I'm hardly gothic-looking.

My mother: Gothic, rock-and-roll. I don't know what your look is. And you're not married and you don't have children, so what can I do? I'm just trying to make you sensible. You can't wait too long. It's very risky, and as you get older it becomes more difficult to conceive.

Me: I don't care about getting married. As far as I'm concerned, getting married isn't all that interesting of a thing to do.

My mother: Here we go with the "interesting." What is interesting to you? Shopping?

Me: Lots of things are interesting. Getting married isn't one of them, though.

My mother: Well, I think it is.

Me: Well, I guess it's a good thing you're married, then. You might want to consider taking note of the fact that marriage is an institution designed to perpetuate a very particular social, religious, and economic system. Personally, I find the whole concept offensive.

My mother: Not getting married is offensive. It's disrespectful for a couple to not get married.

Me: Half of the time, people who get married wind up getting divorced, so what difference does it make? You're a total philistine. Look at your sister, she's been married three times.

My mother: This is what concerns me. My sister is out of her mind.

Me: Your sister is an animal.

My mother: Very nice.

Me: She *is* an animal.

My mother: My sister doesn't know what she's talking about, but it's true she doesn't even think it's necessary to be polite.

Me: So why can't I say she's an animal?

My mother: Because you're not supposed to say something like that about your aunt. It's a terrible thing to say about someone.

Me: I mean it in a very loving way. She wouldn't care anyway. It's not like she's shy.

My mother: She's certainly not shy, but I don't want you to say that about her, it's not nice. Can't you think of a different term?

Me: That's the most accurate one. How else are you supposed to describe someone who takes out a picture of her cat and starts screaming in the middle of a crowded restaurant, "I love my pussy, I have the most beautiful pussy in the entire world"?

My mother: She did that? I can't believe she did that. You're making that up.

Me: I'm not making it up. She did do that.

My mother: That is really awful. There's something wrong with her. There really is. Anyway, I'm very proud of you, but I'm not pleased. I think it's terrible that you're not married. I would be very happy if you were married and settled.

Me: I *am* settled.

My mother goes, look, I love you to pieces and you're the best thing in the world, but it's not easy being your mother, because you don't do anything in a conventional way.

Me: I never got a tattoo.

My mother: That's the only thing. That's the only thing you ever did out of consideration for me. That and not joining the Israeli army. Those are the only things, which is terrible. You can't plan anything with you, it's terrible.

Me: I was delirious when I wanted to join the Israeli army. I was also, like, seventeen years old. And what are you talking about with planning? What do you want to plan?

My mother: I would like to know, for example, that I will go with you one day to buy a wedding gown. And also, I would like to have grandchildren.

Me: If I did believe in getting married, which I don't, I doubt you'd want to go with me to buy my wedding gown. I would wear black.

My mother: OH, NO. You see? That's what I mean. Everything is backwards with you. Why in the world would you wear a black dress?

Me: Because I like black dresses. Plus, I'm not a virgin.

My mother: So?

Me: You're supposed to be a virgin. You were a virgin.

My mother: Yes, I was.

Me: How old were you when you got married?

My mother: Twenty-three.

Me: That's really unbelievable.

My mother: It wasn't so unusual for those days.

Me: Well, had you ever hooked up with anyone?

My mother: What is "hooked up"?

Me: I don't know, had you ever been naked with anyone?

My mother: No. I had never been naked with anyone.

Me: That's really unbelievable. Nobody had ever gone down on you?

My mother: *Went down on me?* Oh my god. No.

Me: No?

My mother: No. I wanted to be pure. I was also very naive, what can I tell you?

Me: So you had no idea what you were doing.

My mother: Papa had many affairs before me, and he was a very good teacher.

Me: That's, like, really more information than I need.

My mother puts the phone down and I hear her go to my father, Michael, I just told Peri that you were a very good teacher in bed, and she said that's more information than she needs. But whether someone "went down on me" before we got married isn't too much information.

I hear my father say, in the voice he uses when he pretends the dog is talking to him, Mommy was a real slut.

needless to say, my mother was very pleased when I got offered a job teaching philosophy to high school students in a summer arts program at a college considered one of the "Little Ivies." The fact that it was, essentially, a glorified summer camp was beside the point. The point was that it was a paid teaching job through an accredited university and, in that, something remotely conventional. Never mind that I didn't know shit about the Greeks. That was inconsequential, this was going to be a contemporary philosophy course.

Along with the other teachers, I arrived on campus before the students, for a week of "staff orientation," which began with a daily staff meeting. This was day two. It was early morning—before nine—all dewy and disgusting out, and I was vicious. I was vicious in part because I don't like to have to get up at that hour, but more important, because I had not yet consumed my daily dose of double espresso with a splash of two-percent milk. Or more to the point, I was vicious because I was being given no indication that there was any chance I was going to get my double espresso with a splash of two-percent milk. As far as I could tell, there were no espresso bars on this campus. What the fuck is the point of being somewhere if I can't have my double espresso with a splash of two-percent milk? This was what I was thinking when someone on a bicycle rolled up next to me.

I look at this person on a bicycle, and she looks like a model from the 1920s. Sexy in a very proper kind of way. Or rather, giving the impression of being proper. I have since learned that this is a false impression, and one, I might add, that she has cultivated to near perfection. Kat is a total con artist. She also happens to have a very cute lisp.

So how are you? she chirps, straddling her bicycle.

I'm terrible, if you must know. I don't know why I said that. Usually I would just say *fine* and be done with the whole thing because what I really wanted was to be left the fuck alone. But I did say that, and sure enough, my response initiated a whole conversation about the fact that I hadn't had my coffee yet.

I should have specified and said espresso, but I didn't, and as a result, Kat pedaled away only to reappear shortly thereafter with a cup of coffee for herself and a gift for me.

A gift.

A gift is a very complicated and, often, very problematic thing.

The problem with a gift is that it is not a mutual exchange. I mean, the thing about a gift is that it's not something you asked for. The act of giving a gift is, among other things, an act of aggression. And it's an act of aggression because the nature of a gift is that you are forced to accept it and then you owe something. People give you a gift because they want something in return.

What Kat wanted was for me to notice her. And this

was her way of courting me. So she presented me with a glass bottle filled with brown sugary liquid that Starbucks tries to pass off as some sort of coffee beverage. Looks like coffee, tastes like cake. I had tasted this concoction once, years earlier. And let me tell you—it's fucking revolting. And even though it was manipulative, it was, on some level, a sweet thing for her to have done, so I took a sip, pretended to be thrilled, and then schlepped the bottle around for the next twenty-some-odd minutes before discreetly throwing it away. It was a very nice gesture on her part, very thoughtful, and also very manipulative. I mean, Kat's not stupid. But then again, neither am I.

a week or so later, I am standing in front of my dormitory in the dark. Like soldiers in barracks, we were quartered away in these four-story cinder-block buildings, three of them surrounding a little grassy quad. For my part, I am waiting for the kids to go to sleep so I can sneak behind the bell tower in the quad for a nicotine fix.

I have to wait for the kids to go to sleep on account of

it being some kind of a cardinal sin to smoke in front of them. Which is fucking absurd. First of all, it's not like I'm living with adolescents. I'm dealing with six-teen- and seventeen-year-olds, and half of them smoke themselves. Second of all, I reek. I mean, I don't smell like a gambling addict who chain-smokes and sets the bed on fire, but I smoke, so I smell like cigarette smoke. I know this. I also know the kids know I smoke, and I'd prefer to acknowledge this rather than pretend I don't smoke, all the while knowing that they know I smoke and that they know that I know they know I smoke.

But none of this matters. Smoking in front of the kids has been deemed unacceptable. So I have to wait. So I'm waiting. And itching. Suddenly, in the darkness, I feel someone hovering over me like a fucking specter.

Here she is again. Kat goes, what are you doing?

What am I doing? I'm standing. That's what I'm doing. I'm waiting to smoke a cigarette.

In response to which Kat says, why don't you just come smoke a cigarette in my room? I raised my eye-brows when Kat said this, but like I said, it was dark, so no one saw me raise my eyebrows. Only I knew that I had raised my eyebrows.

I gave pause. Even more explicit than the no smoking in front of the kids was the no-smoking-in-the-dorms policy.

I followed Kat into her room and she shut the lights off.

Why are you shutting off the lights?

So that no one sees us smoking, she said, crossing through the outer "office" of her little suite—which, come fall term, would, I suspected, be crammed with at least three coeds. I followed her into the smaller room, the one with the bed in it, and sat down. She opened the window above her bed, which looked straight out onto the quad at ground level, which is where we were.

This, I thought, was very suspect. Not the smoking part, but the whole thing that was going on with the bed and the lights off and, basically, the vibe I was getting, which I interpreted as a setup for seduction. All things considered, I was prepared for the possibility of being seduced. I mean, obviously, if I hadn't been prepared, I wouldn't have followed a virtual stranger into her room, allowed all the lights to be turned off, and sat down next to her on her bed.

As aggressive as I am, I have never actually made the first move on anyone. My ego is simply too large to risk it. Only once was I fully the aggressor, and it was with a beautiful young cellist. I had somehow managed to lure her to my apartment, and when we got there, I said take your pants off. The whole thing worked out well enough, but that was a long time ago.

So there I was, sitting on Kat's bed in the dark, wondering if and, if so, how she was going to make a move, when I edged over and felt something poke my behind. I assumed it was a vibrator, because what else would a person have jammed in between her sheets, I unearthed it. But it was not a vibrator. It was a book.

What's this? I asked.

Kat goes, it's a book.

I was like, yes, thank you, I'm aware that something of this size and shape usually indicates "book." What book?

And Kat was like, it's the Book of Mormon.

I nearly fell off the fucking bed. I was like, excuse me? what? I mean, really, who ever heard of someone having the Book of Mormon? And then, I figured she must be kidding. So I go, you're kidding, right?

She wasn't kidding.

Talk about *the wrong impression*. So there I am again, sitting on Kat's bed in the dark, staring out the window and wondering how the fuck I'm supposed to get out of there. I'm thinking, obviously, this is not going to work. I am looking out the window thinking, obviously, this is never going to work, when I spy a small red ember and smoke. And crouched behind, a small figure near the bell tower. Mari. Pronounced *mah*-dee. I spell out her name phonetically in part because there is no way to know that a name spelled "Mari" is pronounced *mah*-dee and also because I would like to make it clear that I don't have any friends named Mary. I try to avoid people named Mary, while Kat, on the other hand, probably tries to *surround* herself by people named Mary. Why? Because Mary was the mother of Jesus, and Kat likes Jesus.

I pressed my face against the screen and whispered, Mah-dee. Much the way Kat had been busy wooing me with syrupy coffee and now this smoke in the dark of her bedroom, I had been trying to work my own magic with Mari. Mari, for her part, is sleek and smooth, with jet-black spiky hair. She is tiny and wild and olive-skinned, and she has those incredible eyes people have when they are half Asian and half something else, which makes a good deal of sense since Mari *is* half Asian and half something else. Japanese and Italian, to be precise.

I was the one teaching philosophy, Kat was the one

teaching journalism, and Mari was teaching architecture and fashion design. And while she had all the discipline and drive of an architect, she also had the most amazing sense of style I'd ever seen. She would wear these T-shirts she made out of boys' undershirts, all stitched up with snaps and asymmetric lines. I *loved* them. And I told her so, but she gets kind of cagey when you compliment her. As much of an egomaniac as I am, Mari is very modest.

So in the dark, by the bell tower, Mari hears her name and looks up. But it's dark, so she doesn't know where it's coming from.

Louder, then. Mah-dee.

Now she looks genuinely perplexed. So I yank up the screen, and louder than I mean to, go, HI!

Mari shoots up from her crouching position, sees me, and starts cracking up. When Mari cracks up—which is fairly often—she really cracks up. I mean, the girl looks like she's having fucking convulsions. She's very animated to begin with, and when she laughs it all becomes exaggerated. She's like, what the hell are you doing? Where are you? I thought it was the director or something and I was getting in trouble for smoking.

I was like, we're in Kat's room.

Then, zeroing in on us, she goes, you're smoking inside?

I look past the Mormon Bible to Kat, and go, it was her idea.

And for the first time in what would turn out to be hundreds, if not thousands, of times, Kat starts laughing a little and goes, Oh, Periel, come on. "Oh, come on" would be Kat's signature line every time there was any sort of disagreement about anything. But it would be some time (and what would turn out to be hundreds, if not thousands, of disagreements) before I would know that.

Mari walks around to the building entrance and disappears.

Kat picks up the Book of Mormon from her bed and a sheet of paper falls out. She doesn't notice. I pick it up to hand to her, and unsure if I want to know what it is, I look anyway.

It's a poem.

Oh god, a *Mormon* poem?

No, not a Mormon poem. An excerpt from Walt Whitman's *Leaves of Grass*.

Hmmmph, I say, not realizing I said hmmmph out loud.

What? says Kat.

Nothing. Nothing, I didn't say anything.

But what I was thinking was, maybe this girl's not so bad after all.

Mari walks in. She is small, but always smoldering with ideas, so her presence is actually quite large.

I give Mari a kiss hello and say, did you know Kat's a Mormon?

Mari goes, she is? You are? Did you go on a mission?

And Kat very nonchalantly, as if this is the most normal thing in the entire world, goes, yeah, in Switzerland. Not only was Kat Mormon, but she had been a Mormon missionary for eighteen months. Which is, seriously, the most berserk thing I had ever heard in my life. I had seen and done some pretty wild shit in my life, but this was enough to put me over the edge.

Perhaps sensing this, Mari whips out a bottle of Maker's Mark from her bag, and the three of us head up to my room on the fourth floor so I can get a few things together before we proceed into the forest for drinks. While I'm in the little office room, Kat closes my bedroom door, and next thing I know, she emerges, dressed up like me, and Mari begins convulsing with laughter on the bed. And what I mean when I say dressed up like me is that Kat's wearing the very outfit I was wearing on the first day of orientation, at the initial staff meeting where we all sat in a circle and said where we were from, what we were teaching, and so on. The day before she bestowed her syrupy gift upon me.

I had been wearing a very typical Periel outfit that I wore, with slight variations, that whole summer. A pair of cutoff camouflage army shorts with an old long-sleeved Motley Crüe T-shirt (obviously it was old, it's not like I would wear a fucking new one), large silver hoop earrings with my name in Hebrew letters, and Gucci sunglasses that I bought at Loehmann's in Los Angeles for forty-nine dollars—I'm not a sucker. I don't shop retail. So, Gucci sunglasses perched on top of my head, as they often are, and black flip-flops. And also a cup that contained a double espresso with a splash of two-percent milk.

So there's Kat, with the whole getup, down to the coffee cup. I'm staring at Kat, about to say something, when she goes, really slowly and all drawn out, because apparently this is how I talk: I'm Periel and I'm teaching philosophy and all of you guys are full of fucking shit.

Obviously, I didn't say that last part, but according to Kat, I may as well have. Kat was cracking up, and Mari was taking pictures of Kat cracking up all dressed up like me—another of Mari's compulsions, besides shirts and blueprints, was her digital camera. The two of them were really howling away.

I was like, very funny. I was like, aren't you guys clever. But actually, I didn't mind. I knew I had to pretend to mind, or they might have stopped. And why would I want them to stop? I mean, I was flattered. It seemed from her doing something like that, I mean, taking note of all the details and taking the time to get all dressed up like that, that Kat admired me, and I was charmed.

Then we got wasted. The night turned into the middle of the night and the middle of the night turned into dawn, and we finally said our good-byes, and with the half-empty (or half-full, depending on your disposition) bottle of liquor Mari had told me to hold on to, I stumbled down to the computer lab in the basement of the dorm. In a very drunken but dedicated fashion, I "surfed the Web" and located what I needed for my students. I printed it out and climbed the stairs to the fourth floor, where I crumpled into bed at about five in the morning.

Once the kids arrived, our staff meetings changed from nine a.m. to eleven a.m. every day, which was certainly better, but still not late enough if you go to bed at five in the morning. My alarm, if I ever set it, didn't wake me. I am also reasonably certain that the fact that I had consumed a good deal of alcohol the previous evening had something to do with why I missed the staff meeting, but either way.

What did wake me up was a thunderous pounding on my door. I hear the pounding and understand that this sound corresponds to the fact that there is someone outside my door who wants to get in, and I stumble to the door, naked.

Mari and Kat are at the door, unfazed that I am naked. I am usually naked. Whenever I have the opportunity to be naked, I take it. I like being naked, it makes me feel very bohemian.

I have a headache, I say, starting to put on a tank top and boxer shorts.

Mari and Kat are looking at me in a way that communicates what I take as a combination of amusement and a good deal of admiration. Judging by the looks on their faces, I thought, these guys really admire me.

Not too much later I discovered that I had misinterpreted the looks on their faces. What they were thinking was not, *we admire you*, but rather, *man, are you in deep shit*. What they were really thinking was, you really fucked up, Periel.

I was like, what? You guys admire me, don't you? I was like, you guys admire me and you want to be like me. You want to fashion yourselves in my likeness. You admire me and you are envious that you are not me.

Kat was like, someone brought up something kind of interesting at staff meeting, which, by the way, you missed.

Me (distracted because I was looking at myself in the mirror and stretching and watching myself stretch, and thinking about the sculpted bodies of the hordes of gay men in ancient Greece; distracted, and therefore not really paying attention to what Mari and Kat were saying, because I was too busy admiring the muscles in my arms and shoulders, thinking, I work hard for this body): Oh yeah?

Them: Yeah. They said that someone left a bottle of

Maker's Mark in the computer lab and that one of the kids found it.

Me (no longer distracted): What? Shit. Are you fucking serious? Oh no. I can't believe this.

Them (evidently enjoying this): Actually, they were pretty cool about the whole thing.

Me: What does that mean, they were pretty cool about it? What did they say?

Them: Actually, it was the last thing brought up. We talked about all sorts of other things, and then something was said to the effect that someone had left an open bottle of Maker's Mark in the computer lab and how, at like six in the morning, the kids who were on Breakfast Club duty with Nico found it.

Me: So Nico found it?

Them: Well, the kids did, but they brought it to him.

Me: Thank god it was Nico.

I said thank god it was Nico, because I knew that Nico wouldn't really give a shit about something like that. Especially since he may well have still been drunk himself from the night before. I said thank god it was Nico, because Nico is totally irresponsible and could have very feasibly done the same thing himself. I said thank god it was Nico, because at the very least Nico is gay and, theoretically at least, that alone makes him more palatable than the assistant program director, Spencer, who is so fucking straight that his mere presence is enough to make you want to put your head through a pane of glass.

Me: So what did Nico say?

Them: He didn't say anything. Spencer was the only one who said anything.

Me: Well, what did *he* say?

Them: Something about gross negligence and about how if something had happened to one of the kids [it always went back to the kids dying], then the insurance wouldn't cover it.

Of course Spencer said that. Spencer was twenty-two years old and very dull. He had just gotten his bachelor's degree from Yale, where he was getting groomed to start law school in the fall at Harvard. Spencer was one of those guys who would be all businesslike and professional during the day, and then, come night, revert to his real self, which entailed slugging back shot after shot of cheap liquor, hitting on anything with a pussy, and just generally acting like a total fraternity guy.

Nico, at least, was consistent about behaving like a rogue. For all of his faults, I appreciated this about him. This and, of course, the fact that he was gay. Not that I like gays across the board, but still, there's something to be said for having to come out. The trauma of it builds character.

Nico may have been a rogue, but Spencer, like most fraternity guys, was an asshole. Why are most fraternity guys assholes? Because they're groomed to behave like rapists, that's why. Because they walk around with wads of daddy's money shoved up their asses and they think they can do whatever the fuck they want because they've always been able to do whatever the fuck they want because they're spoiled little shits.

Among the social elite and, indeed, in large part among people who belong to things like fraternities and yacht clubs, there is a prevailing ethos, an unspoken, odious understanding. These people buy their way into little groups so that they can be surrounded by other people who can also afford to buy their way into groups so that they do not have to interact with people who cannot afford to associate with them. This is *gross*. Their unspoken understanding is that you are worthy of being part of their group only if you can afford to be. They insulate themselves because they want to be safe. They insulate themselves because it makes them *feel* safe. Of course, they are *not* safe. They do everything in their power to pretend that a deep, dark fear does not lurk inside them. This is why, for example, they line up like sheep to become part of the status quo. This is why they act in a "professional" manner. This is why Spencer acts like a businessman during the day, and then at night becomes intoxicated and behaves like a fucking beast.

Spencer may not be a shitty human being (though more likely than not, he is), but he certainly lives his life as a person who acts as though he is very concerned with "the rules," because he wants to "make it."

There's a difference between being ambitious, which is fine, and wanting to "make it." The difference between the two comes down to motivation. Like, what's motivating you? And if it's money that's motivating you, you're a selfish, greedy piece of shit. You want to be a lawyer? Good for you, maybe you can do something helpful in this world. You're going to make money too? Good for you again, I'm certainly not suggesting everyone needs to live like a fucking ascetic. But if you want to be a lawyer because you want to buy a helicopter and a house in the Hamptons, personally, I want nothing to do with you. Would you want your doctor to be a person who became a doctor just because he wanted to get rich? I certainly fucking wouldn't. I would want my doctor to be a person who is motivated by higher aspirations.

I don't know whether Spencer was going to law school for a helicopter, but I suspected so, and I thought he might take this whole Maker's Mark episode very seriously.

Me: Do you think I'm going to get fired?

Them: They don't know it was you, P.

When I finally found Spencer, he was wearing a short-sleeved Polo shirt and a pair of mirrored sunglasses. I wanted to be like, *nice shirt, dude,* but instead I was like, look, Spencer, I just want to apologize for leaving that bottle in the computer lab. I realize the gravity of the situation and what could have potentially occurred.

And Spencer, who had been drinking with us less than a week earlier (and more or less trying to get into my pants), looks at me—or I think he's looking at me; with those mirrored sunglasses, who can tell?—and he gets like all serious and goes, well, just as long as you realize the gravity of the situation and, er, uh, well, what could have potentially occurred.

I was like—but I didn't say this—are you a fucking moron? Obviously I realize the fucking gravity of the situation, I just fucking said I realized the gravity of the situation. If you're going to fucking reprimand me, do you think you could do it without repeating what I just said, verbatim?

I mean, really.

And this was one of the problems with this program. People were idiots. That and Breakfast Club.

Breakfast Club was how the kids got punished when they did something "wrong." What did that mean? It meant, for example, not being in your room by eleven-thirty at night; there were all sorts of reasons the kids got Breakfast Club duty. And it entailed waking up at the ass-crack of dawn and going with Nico to pick up litter around campus or in the computer lab—in which case you were liable to find a half-empty bottle of bourbon, compliments of Periel.

For my part, I found the whole concept pretty offensive. First, the name alone made me cringe. Second, I have absolutely no idea how or why anyone ever expected to get teenagers to behave a certain way by threatening them with something called "Breakfast Club." I mean, give me a fucking break. I'm so sure anyone saying the words, "You have Breakfast Club," is going to be taken seriously. That in and of itself seems so obvious. How are you going to invoke the phrase "Breakfast Club" and expect to be taken seriously? And beyond that, it's a miserable way to handle a person, teenage or otherwise. I can tell you this much: When I was that age, I was a real wiseass, and had anyone told me I had Breakfast Club, I would have laughed in their fucking face.

I, obviously, never gave anyone Breakfast Club. I can hardly even imagine resorting to something so shameful. And anyway, if any of the kids ever gave me a hard time, it happened exactly once, and then, believe me, it never happened again. I mean, the kids weren't idiots. They knew exactly what they could get away with. And they also knew better than to try and fuck with me. I think it's pretty apparent, even to a fifteen- or sixteen-year-old, that I'm not someone you would choose to have on your bad side. And like I said, the kids weren't idiots. And so they knew that. And I knew, because I am also not an idiot, that if you treat people with respect, you will probably never have to resort to humiliating yourself by saying things like, "You have Breakfast Club."

Kat, of course, never gave anyone Breakfast Club either. But like every staff member, she was responsible for keeping general order on her floor. This meant, among other things, that every night a certain member of the staff—a different one each night, on a rotating schedule—was assigned check-in duty. And what this meant was that every night, the girls, one by one, though sometimes in giggling clusters, would come knock on said staff member's door and be like, I'm here. And you, the person who was doing check-in, would have a list and put a check mark next to each of their names so as to indicate that each girl was, in fact, alive.

Look, I understand that some of these details may be a bit tedious, but you'll have to bear with me if you want to get the story straight. If you're bored by these details, too fucking bad. Herman Melville droned on for like ninety-seven pages in *Moby-Dick* about whale semen, so this really isn't that bad.

As I was saying. It's one in the morning. I'm sitting at my desk in my room doing whatever it is that I do. Writing. Masturbating. Toying with the idea of bugging out. I can't bug out. Why can't I bug out? Because when you're bugging out, you're totally self-absorbed and you can't think of anyone but yourself. This is not a possibility, because, as Kat informs me, when she busts into my room, I need to go to her room so I can help her tend to Brooke Fenster-Bloom, who really is bugging out.

So there's Kat at my door at one in the fucking morning, all wrapped up in her nightclothes with this dopey look in her eyes. Like the way my dog looks at me when he wants to be fed. That's how Kat was looking at me. Like she wanted something from me and also like she knew she was going to get it.

Kat: Something's wrong with Brooke Fenster-Bloom.

Me: What's wrong with Brooke Fenster-Bloom, other than the fact that she's a snotty bitch?

Kat: She has cramps.

I'm like, o-kay, she has cramps. *And?*

And Kat was like, well . . . And then she sort of shifted around a bit. . . . She has cramps and she's in my room.

I was like, *what?* I was like, what do you mean, *she's in your room?*

You have to understand that, given the context, Brooke Fenster-Bloom's being in Kat's room was really sort of a scandal. To begin with, the kids had no business being in our rooms. And also, it was one in the morning. The kids were supposed to be in their rooms

32

by eleven-thirty. But this night was different because this night, Kat showed up at my door at one in the morning wrapped up like a fucking burrito and told me that instead of Brooke Fenster-Bloom coming to her door for check-in and saying, I'm here, she came to her door and was like, I'm here and I'm fourteen and I have cramps and I miss my mother, who is vacationing at Hilton Head, South Carolina, and also, I'm crying.

And Kat, always the Mormon, took Brooke Fenster-Bloom and wrapped *her* up like a fucking burrito and put her in the extra bed in her room.

Which was well beyond the call of duty. Which was extraordinarily thoughtful. I mean, in a certain respect, all Brooke Fenster-Bloom wanted was to be loved. And Kat, the consummate do-gooder, complied. To the best of her ability, at least. Kat, apparently, deemed herself only moderately competent to deal with this situation. Kat, apparently, felt she was competent enough to deal with the situation only insofar as she was competent enough to gather Brooke Fenster-Bloom, wrap her up like a fucking burrito, put her in the extra bed in her room, and then come get me. Which she did.

She put Brooke Fenster-fucking-Bloom into her extra bed, and then she climbed, with her long, lithe

33

legs, up the stairs to my room. So I had to stop masturbating or toying with the idea of going berserk, or
whatever it was that I was doing, and go downstairs to
Kat's room, where I found Brooke Fenster-Bloom, who
was, and I imagine still is, like six feet tall, lying in the
dark, under like seventeen blankets, on the extra bed in
Kat's room.

Crying. Or sort of weepy.

Kat, at this point, had sunk her long body into a chair
so that she was facing Brooke Fenster-Bloom, who, incidentally, has a pacemaker embedded in her chest.

And there I was. Standing. At the head of the bed.

What's wrong, Brooke? You don't feel well?

Brooke Fenster-Bloom: Uh-uh.

Me: Okay, you have cramps?

Brooke Fenster-Bloom: Uh-huh.

Me: Okay, have you taken any medicine?

Brooke Fenster-Bloom: Uh-huh.

Panic.

What medicine had Brooke Fenster-Bloom taken,
and would it kill her?

Precisely because of a situation like this, we were
not allowed to administer drugs. There was, in fact, only
one staff member—Nico—who *was* allowed to. He was

the only one who was allowed to administer drugs, and he was in charge of the money. This was funny, because as it turned out, Nico was the one staff member who *did* more drugs than the rest of us, and was also the biggest spendthrift I've ever known. This guy would just *hemorrhage* money. And allegedly he pilfered like $6,000 from the program's bank account, but no one knew that yet. In any case, we were not supposed to hand out meds, because when you have a group of students, or any group of people for that matter, you are bound to have a select few who have some heinous medical condition and/or very serious allergies. Most of them don't, but some do, and Brooke Fenster-Bloom was one of those who did. So the situation really could have become catastrophic.

Brooke Fenster-Bloom said yes, she had taken some sort of medication to alleviate her cramps, and yes, she was sure that the medicine she had taken was okay to take.

This was all handled very delicately, you understand. To begin with, it makes for a bit of a strained situation when you know an intimate detail about someone—namely, the fact that she has a pacemaker embedded in her chest—but you really don't know the person about whom you know this detail. All staff members were required to familiarize themselves with all of the students' medical files. Which is to say that everyone, indeed, the entire staff, knew that Brooke Fenster-Bloom had a pacemaker embedded in her chest. But of course Brooke Fenster-Bloom didn't know that everyone knew this. The same way we all knew that Jessica Braun was a self-cutter with purging tendencies.

Anyway, the point being that Brooke Fenster-Bloom was very weepy and the situation had to be handled very delicately and there I was, rising to the occasion and comforting her. I was comforting her because I am Jewish, and Jewish women—even though I adamantly reject being categorized in such a fashion—have a gene or something that renders them very nurturing. I reject this. I reject all of this. I reject being categorized as "woman," because if I am to conceive of myself as "woman," then I subscribe to the political regime Monique Wittig calls heterosexuality. And I do not.

Nevertheless, there I was at one o'clock in the fucking morning, filling up a balloon with hot water so that Brooke Fenster-Bloom could place it on her abdomen to help relieve her cramps. I reject those ways of being categorized, yet when duty called, there I was, telling Brooke Fenster-Bloom one thing after another to try to get her mind off the fact that she had cramps and missed her mother, who was probably at a beach resort somewhere, sucking down a gin fizz.

It should be said that, pacemaker aside, there was something very wrong with Brooke Fenster-Bloom. First, she was a kind of hybrid human being. A half-breed, so to speak: half Jew, half Gentile, with neither parent particularly interested in his or her respective religion or, for that matter, in Brooke - Fenster-Bloom. As a result, Brooke Fenster-Bloom had become something of a painfully precocious religious fundamentalist.

How did I know this?

Because one of the first things Brooke Fenster-Bloom told me when I met her was that she had recently broken up with her boyfriend of four years. She said, I realize this is sort of an unusual thing, considering my age and all, and it's not that I don't care for him any longer, but well, the whole thing was quite difficult.

Naturally, I asked her why they had broken up, at which point Brooke Fenster-Bloom, who, I'd like to remind you, is *fourteen*, informed me that the fact that her boyfriend did not believe in egalitarian services had become an insurmountable problem.

Egalitarian?

It's worth pointing out that Brooke Fenster-Bloom is the same girl who, on one of the first days of the program, announced to me that she wanted to arrange a minyan.

A minyan, incidentally, is some prayer thing that fanatic Jews do. They get together at temple, and they do this prayer thing, and in order to do it they need ten men. It has to be ten and it has to be men. It always has to be ten men, and without the requisite ten men you can't do it. But Brooke Fenster-Bloom, in her gender-forward thinking, wanted to do this with mixed-gender teenagers.

I was like, I really don't know, Brooke. This isn't a religious program. I mean, if there are services here on campus and you wanted to *attend* them, maybe you could do that, but I don't think the program is going to actually organize it.

Brooke Fenster-Bloom glared at me.

I happened to notice, she said, that you have your name written in Hebrew across your earrings.

I was like, yes, Brooke, I do have my name written in Hebrew across my hoop earrings, but I don't really see what that has to do with anything.

Brooke Fenster-Bloom continued to glare at me. Well, she said, aren't *you* Jewish?

I tried to hedge. It didn't work. So I acquiesced. Yes, Brooke, I'm Jewish, but like I said, I don't really see what that has to do with anything.

Brooke Fenster-Bloom bears down on me and goes, I'm just asking if you go to temple.

I was like, fine. Okay. No. I do not go to temple.

Brooke Fenster-Bloom: Why not?

Oy.

Because, Brooke Fenster-Bloom, for me, being Jewish is more of a cultural thing than a religious thing. Because I think identifying solely with religion, rather than with the culture or traditions of a religion, draws people apart, highlights their differences instead of bringing them together. And anyway, I'm Israeli and, contrary to popular belief, most Israelis are secular.

Brooke Fenster-Bloom goes, so you don't believe in God?

I hedged again and went to find Kat, to tell her how

Brooke Fenster-Bloom had been grilling me. I was like, Kat, Brooke Fenster-Bloom has obviously been indoctrinated. Or brainwashed. Or both.

Kat goes: Oh, Periel, come on. What does a fourteen-year-old know about God?

Seriously, Kat. Please. There is obviously something very wrong when you have a fourteen-year-old who talks more about God than she talks about anything else. I mean, *what the fuck can a fourteen-year-old know about God?* Can you answer that question for me, please?

Kat goes, Joseph Smith, the first prophet of the Mormon Church, was fourteen when he had his first vision.

I was like, no, Kat. That is not the answer. The answer is that a fourteen-year-old knows as much about God as the rest of us. Which is nothing. You can't be that sure of anything—it's totally fucking arrogant *and* the reasoning is flawed. You can't be so sure of anything, let alone something you have no way of knowing anything about. If you even want to pretend to take yourself seriously as an intellectual, you can't believe in nonsense like god and like "heaven."

Kat goes, I believe in heaven.

I was like, Kat, let me tell you something. And listen very carefully. If you want to go to heaven, you should go to that strip club in Los Angeles I was telling you about, and you should wear a skirt with no underwear and do yourself a favor. Get a lap dance from that stripper with all the tattoos, I think her name is Jade. She'll blow on your coochie. Do that, you'll be in heaven. Believe me.

While I was considering murdering Kat for luring me into this whole cramps situation, I thought it would be a good time to revisit this topic. I was desperate for Brooke Fenster-Bloom to go to sleep, and so instead of working her up and answering the God question myself, I was like, Brooke, you know, Kat believes in God. She thinks God has a long white beard and is sitting on a cloud watching us. And she thinks that when you die, you go to heaven.

Kat looked like she was going to rip my head off.

I could barely contain myself. I went on. I was like, I don't know if you know this or not, Brooke, but Kat's a Mormon. Not a moron, Brooke, a Mormon.

Brooke Fenster-Bloom had propped herself up in bed at this point, and suddenly her eyes got wide and glassy.

I go, right, Kat?

It should be noted that Kat's eyes, like Brooke Fenster-Bloom's eyes, were very wide, though not glassy.

I was like, this is really wild, so get ready: The Mormons believe that there are three levels of heaven.

The third, and lowliest, level is the *telestial* level. It's where you go if you sin *sometimes* but you also go to church regularly and pay your tithes. Paying your tithes, incidentally, means that you donate ten percent of your annual income to the Church of Scientology. I mean, the Mormon Church of Latter-day Saints. Whatever. Same difference. You can't talk to God, but you can hear Him, and you can see Him. It's kind of like you're watching God on TV, which is why it has the prefix *tele*.

Kat went totally berserk after I said "same difference" about Scientology and Mormonism. She was like, Periel, this is the most ridiculous thing I've ever heard in my entire life.

I ignored her.

The second level, *Brooke*, is the *terrestrial* level, and it is where you go if you sin *rarely* but go to church regularly and pay your tithes. In the second level, you can hear God *and* you can talk to Him. This is for the Mor-

mons who are more down-to-earth, hence, the incorpo-
ration of the prefix *terre,* which comes from the Latin
for "earth."

And finally there is the first, and best, level. To get
into the first level, which is the *celestial* level, you must essentially be perfect. You *never* sin, you go to church regularly, and you pay your tithes. In this case, you can hear
Him, talk to Him, and you're standing smack in front of
Him. I imagine you can also smell Him and brush His
hair if you want to. This level is obviously the most
exciting—let's say it's akin to a VIP room, which is why
it starts off with the same prefix as the word *celebrity.*

I was like, you should know that Kat didn't tell me
any of this—I got all this information from a third
party. Apparently the Mormons run a tight ship, and
this information is not handed out freely. My question
is, are there front-row seats? Or is everyone standing?
Either way, doesn't the front row fill up pretty quickly?
I mean, how many people can be standing, or even sitting, in front of God at any given moment? If level one
reaches capacity, then what? And who gets to decide
this, anyway?

Kat, who was getting a little uppity, goes, please,
Periel, that's ridiculous.

Listen, Brooke, Kat has corroborated this next part. Apparently, if you do go to church regularly and you do pay your tithes, you get a "temple recommend" card, which grants you entrance into all the best restaurants in Salt Lake City and can also double as a Blockbuster card.

Kat: Periel, that is such a twisted thing to say.

Let me tell you something, Brooke Fenster-Bloom, I am *scandalized* by this. To think that thousands and thousands of people are flocking to this fucking church trying to get into a level of heaven that doesn't exist is scandalous. I was like, insofar as I'm concerned, the Mormon missionaries are like serial killers in that they prey on people weaker than themselves. These missionaries try to get their claws into people who have lost all hope. How can anyone tolerate this?

I said this, but interestingly enough, not only do I tolerate Kat, but I adore her. This is interesting because I usually loathe people who are into religion. Of course— and Kat isn't too pleased to hear this—truth be told, Kat really isn't *all* that into religion, even though there are all sorts of things she says and does that might lead you to believe she is. For instance, in the 1970s, her great-grandfather was the prophet of the Mormon Church, which as far as I can tell is akin to being the pope. So her great-grandfather was essentially the Mormon pope, and also her great-great-great-great-grandfather had some crazy name like Heber, had around fifty-seven wives, and was a big-shot Mormon in his own right.

Brooke Fenster-Bloom goes: My stomach hurts. I want to call my mother.

I go, I want to call my mother too, but it's much too late for either of us. Believe me, I tell her, I can relate. Once when I was your age, my stomach hurt too. I got my period at my uncle Mark's house and I didn't have tampons, so I screamed down the stairs, "DOES ANY-ONE HAVE A TAMPON?" And Uncle Mark totally freaked out and said he didn't want to hear about me getting my period. At which point I started screaming and bugging out. Similar to how you are bugging out now, except I was a lot more aggressive than you are.

I was so angry at Uncle Mark that I marched down-stairs with a wad of toilet paper in my underwear and was like, excuse me, but I'll have you know that I get my period once a month and so does your wife and so does your daughter and so does every single other fucking female on the face of the planet. Once every month, the lining of my uterus falls out, sometimes in chunks, and if you don't like it, too fucking bad.

My mother was like, *Peri, please, do you have to use such language?* But I was on such a tirade I didn't care. Can you imagine the audacity of trying to make it seem like getting your period is something unmentionable? This was years ago—like I said, back when I was your age, but it was still the modern age. Uncle Mark is much more comfortable discussing such things now, and for many years after the whole fiasco, I would call him every month to let him know when I was menstruating.

Brooke Fenster-Bloom was sitting there with her mouth half open, kind of amused maybe, but also more like: My parents wouldn't approve of this—at all.

I look over at Kat, who was sitting there like a fucking librarian but who seemed notably relieved that I had stopped talking about Mormonism.

Are you tired yet? I asked Brooke Fenster-Bloom.

Brooke Fenster-Bloom responded that, no, she was not yet feeling the nudge of sleep coming on. And then, clearly still stuck on the three levels of heaven, she asked me (again) if I believed in God.

I acquiesced. I said: The problem, Brooke Fenster-

Bloom, is that I don't like talking about God, because when you're talking about God, you don't really *know* anything. No offense, but no one really knows anything. The pope knows that God doesn't exist. That's the secret of his fucking power.

Kat, suddenly perking up at the sound of heresy, goes, Periel, *please*.

I go, don't give me that "Periel, please" shit, Jean Baudrillard said that. In *Seduction*. And you'd know that if you'd read *Seduction*. And you probably would have read *Seduction* if you weren't so busy reading the fucking Bible. Don't look at me like that, Kat, I know what I'm talking about. And if you don't believe me, you can check for yourself: "Thus the Pope, the Grand Inquisitor, the great Jesuits and theologians all knew that God did not exist; this was their secret, and the secret of their strength." Page sixty-fucking-six.

Kat goes: Maybe if you weren't so busy reading Baudrillard, you'd have read the fucking Bible.

Brooke Fenster-Bloom gave a big laugh at this.

I said, listen, Brooke Fenster-Bloom, I'm a neopragmatist in the Singerian tradition of neopragmatism. Essentially, what I believe in is the reduction of suffering. Peter Singer is one of the greatest philosophers of our time, and his philosophy, I would argue, is pretty on the money. I agree with what he says, that each of us is responsible for the reduction of suffering to the extent that by reducing the suffering of someone else, we do not ourselves suffer *more than* or *as much as* the person whose suffering we are attempting to reduce. He talks about proximity. Like, just because someone is starving, homeless, gravely ill, or whatever, in, for example, Africa, which is pretty fucking far away, we are no less responsible for reducing that person's suffering. Provided, of course, that making the person suffer less wouldn't make us suffer more.

Brooke Fenster-Bloom was like, huh?

I was unmoved. I can't dumb things down any more than this. I forged ahead.

Peter Singer is also very controversial. He supports euthanasia for infants who are born with things like spina bifida, and when he got hired to teach at Princeton, there was a huge uproar by this group of disabled people called Not Dead Yet. They were all up in arms— or at least some of them were, some of them probably didn't have arms—but either way, they were super-pissed that he got hired, because, they said, according to his philosophy, they should have all been killed at birth. Which isn't exactly true, his words always get misconstrued, but in any event, some people think he's a hypocrite because he says shit like that, like that *quality* of life is more important than *being* alive, and then he goes ahead and keeps his mother, who is like a hundred ten years old and very sick, alive for ages when he could have just let her die.

Brooke Fenster-Bloom, meanwhile, had fallen into an advanced state of REM. It was Singerian neopragmatism at its best: everyone's suffering had been reduced.

Suddenly all schmaltzy, Kat walked me back upstairs to my room, showering me with hugs and thank yous. She can be sentimental as fucking hell, and she's always worrying about the way people feel, which is tedious but also nice at the same time. She also has an enormous sense of guilt, and it's usually for the most ridiculous things. One time, after the affair with Brooke Fenster-Bloom, she and I were driving around in one of the vans that we toted the kids around in, except there were no kids in the van when Kat was burning rubber at ninety miles per hour on some highway in Vermont.

Not only did she feel terribly guilty, but she was genuinely shocked that she got pulled over.

Afterward she was basically hanging her head in shame. She was going, oh, Periel, I feel awful. I can't believe I just got a ticket.

I was like, Kat, what do you mean, you can't believe you just got a ticket? You were driving almost double the fucking speed limit.

I just feel so guilty, she announced with her very cute lisp.

Who feels guilty about getting a speeding ticket? I was like, Kat, this is *not* a big deal. This is, like, really not a big deal, and furthermore, this performance you're putting on is really very Gentile of you.

Oh, Periel, come on.

I was like, look, Kat. The Jews don't feel guilty about things like getting tickets. If a Jew speeds and gets a ticket, it's almost like she was expecting it. That's the difference between you and me. Or more precisely, the difference between Gentiles and Jews.

Kat: Periel, please.

Me: No, Kat. It's true. When we Jews do something wrong, we *expect* to get caught. Gentiles think they're going to get away with it, and they're always shocked as hell when they get caught. Why do you think Jews commit so few violent crimes? *You* feel guilty only *because* you got caught. That's bullshit. If we hadn't been pulled over, you would have raced all the way back to campus driving like a fucking lunatic. If you really meant it, you'd have felt guilty regardless of whether or not you had been pulled over. Or you wouldn't have been speeding to begin with.

another problem: Everyone at this program was operating under the assumption that the kids needed to be entertained, like, twenty-four hours a day. This is false. People do not need to be entertained with mindless garbage twenty-four hours a day. In fact, not only do people not need to be entertained with mindless garbage twenty-four hours a day, but they shouldn't be.

This being the case, I had big problems the day we took the kids to Boston, which was about five hours from where we were. Because there were around two hundred students, we had to charter buses and divide everyone up.

I was informed three movies were going to be shown

on the drive there. You don't have to show *three* fucking movies. Showing *three* movies is lazy and irresponsible. The kids should have been encouraged to talk, to ask one another questions about their lives. They should not have been encouraged to zone out in front of a television screen. Five hours is enough time to actually learn something worthwhile. Five hours is enough time to actually do something useful. I was incensed.

I was still figuring out how everything worked. Which is to say that I had no idea that the movie *Shallow Hal* was going to be shown on the bus and proceed to rot our brains. In case you don't know, *Shallow Hal* is an odious movie starring Gwyneth Paltrow and Jack Black. The movie is all about how Jack Black's character makes some promise to his dying father about how he will fall in love only with beautiful women, and thus he falls in love with Paltrow's character. Except Jack Black's character has been brainwashed by Anthony Robbins, the self-help guru, who makes a cameo appearance as himself in the film (and believe me, I'm using the term "film" very loosely), and thus Jack Black's character does not realize that Gwyneth Paltrow's character is fat and ugly. Because he has been brainwashed, he thinks Paltrow's character is thin and beautiful.

The "film," needless to say, was awful. I mean, it was beyond awful. It was totally reprehensible. Why? Well, to start with, because if Gwyneth Paltrow's character had really been black and Jack Black's character had fallen for her because he mistook her for being white, it would have been fucked up, right? Well, same here. Why? Because fat people, like black people, are marginalized. That's why. Because we're taught to hate our bodies if we don't look like supermodels, that's why. Because if you're dealing with teenage girls who already hate their bodies, and even if being as gluttonous as Gwyneth Paltrow's character was in that movie is revolting, there are other, better ways to communicate that message. Instead of showing a busload of teenagers a movie about some bitch who is disgusting because she is fat, show them a movie that condemns the structure that has made her fat. Show them *Super Size Me* instead of *Shallow* fucking *Hal*.

The deal is this: when you are in charge of kids, they look at you. They look at you and they watch you and they take their cues from you. They watch every move you make, they watch you all the time, and it's not like they don't know what's going on. They know exactly what the fuck is going on. When, for example, we show

53

a movie like *Shallow Hal*, they make inductive leaps, like:

(a) Out of the three million movies that exist in the world, we, the teachers, chose this one.

(b) If we chose this movie, we must think this is a good movie, because why would we bother to show a movie we didn't think was good?

(c) This is the level of intelligence we think they are functioning at, that we expect them to function at, or alternatively, this is the level of intelligence we are functioning at.

It seems reasonably clear to me that none of this is very promising. Also, it goes back to the fact that people don't need to be entertained twenty-four hours a day. It's like, okay, big deal, five hours on the bus, big fucking deal. Read a book. Or, whatever, fine, show a movie, I'm not Mussolini, I have no problem showing a film. You want to show a film? Fine. Let's show a film. But let's show a film, then. A smart film. Something that is actually worthwhile. Something that might actually stimulate some mental activity.

So, needless to say, or not needless to say, since I've already said it, this *Shallow Hal* incident really set me off. So I decided that if anything was ever going to get accomplished, I was going to have to take over. It wasn't all that complicated. It went like this: I decided I was going to take over, and then I took over. So maybe I am Mussolini. So what.

In the next staff meeting, I went totally berserk and started ranting and raving, giving my whole above spiel, and then, because nobody wanted to incur the wrath they knew would certainly follow if they tried to fuck with me, they let me take over.

The fact of the matter is, it gets to a point where bitching isn't that interesting. It's like Gore Vidal said: It's always possible to make things better—as well as worse. I decided to make things better. So the next time we took a bus trip, I was armed with a bag of videos checked out from the local indie rental store—Jorge Furtado's *Isle of Flowers*; that great documentary on James Baldwin, *The Price of the Ticket*; *Manhattan*; and *Hedwig and the Angry Inch*. And maybe there was a little grumbling, but only at first.

My success with the *Shallow Hal* episode inspired me to tackle another problem. One night, by the bell tower, which had become our late-night smoking spot,

Mari, Kat, and I were talking about how our female students were prancing around with inane slogans spelled out across their chests, T-shirts that read "Tasty" or "Idaho? No, you da ho" right across their tits.

I was like, the whole point is that people are constantly staring at our tits, right? And people are constantly staring at our tits because our bodies are objectified because our tits are oversexualized, right? It follows, then, that we should take advantage of this fact, right? Mari took a drag of her cigarette and nodded.

I think we should put our tits to better use—it's prime advertising space being wasted on vapid slogans like "Princess." Instead of turning us into a bunch of apathetic morons, T-shirts should say things like: "On any given day in the richest country in the world, there are 600,000 homeless people," or "By 2020, 100 million people in Africa will have died of AIDS."

We should reject renting our bodies as billboard space for odious companies and use them instead to our advantage, to advertise for shit that matters. We should be wearing politically minded clothing, clothes that say things people aren't saying. We should use our tits to make people think about things no one else is making them think about.

If Michael Moore made being politically involved hip, I wanted to make it *sexy*. And look, I'm not jerking myself off here. I wasn't under some delirious impression that I would, like, save the world by making clothes, but at least I'm aware of what's going on.

So shortly thereafter, Mari taught me how to silk-screen. It is a complicated process, silk-screening. To begin with, you have to be at least somewhat competent in drawing in order to paint your design onto a screen. As if that weren't enough, you have to be able to do it backward, because, as it turns out, you have to flip the screen onto the fabric of the shirt. And you have to paint in negative space, whatever that means.

Even after three hours of Mari's patient instructions, I was completely covered in ink. This way, she explained, like a mother hen. No, P, you have to do it the other way. Paint in the negative—a concept I continue to find challenging. Negative space, along with all other abstract concepts, makes perfect sense to Mari, and she was turning out perfect shirts. My words, meanwhile, kept coming up backward. I was trying to make a shirt that said "Foucault is sexy" and instead got "sexy is Foucault." Granted, not the most accessible, but I *like* Foucault and I was in the middle of teaching his work to my students. Not only was he a fierce and radical thinker, he was also a member of the underground gay leather scene in San Francisco in the 1980s, and *that* is certainly sexy.

What's *not* sexy is that in addition to being a fierce and radical thinker, he was also running around knowingly infecting men with HIV. But that's another story (and T-shirt).

Defeated, I showed Mari, who declared "sexy is Foucault" more interesting than "Foucault is sexy." Encouraged by her approval, I forged ahead.

I convinced the program to fork over upward of $800 so I could order the various supplies for the students to design and print their own shirts as an extracurricular activity. Extracurricular activities, mind you, were not only sanctioned; they were virtually the selling point of the program, which passed itself off to parents as enriching, academic, college-résumé material—never mind that these activities generally amounted to paintball and bowling. Spencer droned on and on about how this was too expensive of an activity until I was finally like, look, you spend $400 dollars a week on pizza alone, so give me a fucking break.

He relented.

I gave a special lecture to my students and told them about the project. I spoke to them about responsibility. About how we should think about the fact that a lot of the clothes worn by us in the Western world are made, for example, in Haiti by twelve-year-olds who don't earn in a year what it costs us to buy our fucking underwear. And that the massive corporations that market their brands as sexy are, essentially, sexualizing underage slave labor. And that wearing something like a Nike swoosh across your chest is fucking insidious.

I was very riled up and felt I had hit upon something critical. It was time to raise the stakes. It was time for Larry Kramer.

In the early 1980s, before you were born, I told the students, Larry Kramer was living a fabulous life in New York City. Gay men were running around like wild animals, fucking each other up the ass, and after all those years of it not being okay to be gay, it must have been nice to finally feel free. But it ended almost as quickly and forcefully as it had begun. Suddenly, and seemingly for no reason, all of these beautiful, smart, talented gay young men started coming down with a bizarre and brutal illness, and nobody knew what it was or how to cure it. They were calling it "gay cancer." It was, of course, AIDS.

Thousands of people were dying god-awful deaths, and no one did a goddamn thing. No one wanted to touch it—it was too ugly and totally petrifying. There were no social services, there was no research on this health crisis, and gay men were dropping like flies. Ronald Reagan didn't even *mention* the word "AIDS" publicly until his *sixth* year in office.

But there was one man who was not afraid. Or actually, he was terrified, because he was the first person to realize that this was a pandemic that would reach holocaustic proportions, and the first to *do something* about it.

Larry Kramer. Larry Kramer was like, FUCK THIS. He didn't play by the rules—he didn't play by *anybody's* rules—he did what he knew he had to do to get people to start paying attention.

Naturally, people hated him. I mean, he made them nervous. He said the things everyone else was scared to say and he said them to the people everyone else was afraid to say them to. Someone once approached Larry on the street—I think it was someone he knew from the early 1980s—and the guy said, thanks so much for all the work you have done. And Kramer was like, fuck you, you could have done it too.

I believe Larry Kramer had more of an impact on getting people to pay attention to the fact that thousands of gay men were dying of AIDS than anyone else in the Western world. If people had listened to him, we would probably be living in a very different world. Today, if you can afford the drugs, AIDS is no longer a death sentence. But that's a big *if*. Because more than twenty years later, millions of people are *still* dying of AIDS. Except now they're mostly in Africa.

As people of privilege—and having enough to eat constitutes that—we have the job, indeed, the responsibility, to be aware and to do our part to make others aware.

That said, almost every girl in the program showed up for the T-shirt-making activity, and I knew I was doing something right when one of my students turned out a shirt that read: "Larry Kramer for President." Brooke Fenster-Bloom approached me wearing a shirt that said simply "Rwanda" all over it. She had been inspired by a poster by the Chilean photographer Alfredo Jaar, which was part of an installation of his that I had told the students about called *Let There Be Light: The Rwanda Project*. Her shirt almost made up for the five hours she had tortured me up in Kat's room.

I was thrilled, and when the kids were done, I screened myself a shirt. It turned out perfectly, and read: "the only bush i trust is my own."

Less than two months later, after my respectable job was over, I went back to displeasing my mother by being a poorly paid writer and a well-paid waitress. One day I walked into a chic boutique wearing my new favorite tank top. The owner went totally crazy. She was like, oh my god, the only bush i trust is my own, that is *hilarious*, where did you get that shirt—I have to get some for the store. She was all over me, and finally persuaded me to make her some. I went home and pumped out like ten shirts. I was, once again, completely covered in ink, but the shirts, I thought, looked pretty good. I made little labels for them, and with my newly acquired sewing skills attached them. In honor of my students, I decided to call the clothing line—which I thought of as more of an anti-clothing line—"body as billboard."

The owner of the boutique was delighted to receive her new shirts. Two weeks later, I went back to the store.

There wasn't a shirt in sight. I was like, what happened to all my shirts?

She goes, we're sold out. And I have good news and bad news.

Me: The fact that you're sold out isn't good news?

The owner: Well, that is good news, but we have more good news. And bad news. Which do you want first?

Me: The bad news.

The owner: Someone returned a shirt because the words came out when she washed it.

Me: Too bad. These shirts are like Pop art. They're one-of-a-kind. I paused. I mean, I'll make her a new one. What's the good news?

The owner: Betsey Johnson was just in and she bought the last two shirts we had. And she's having a party at her store tonight. It's a fund-raiser for breast cancer. You should go.

Betsey Johnson. I couldn't fucking believe it.

But seriously, I'm not showing up, uninvited, to Betsey Johnson's breast cancer party. That's absurd.

Kat was like, you're going. Of course you're going.

I was like, I am *not* going.

The owner goes, you don't need an invitation, you should just show up.

Kat goes, *see.*

She hounded me for a while, and finally, I was like, *fine.*

I raced back to my apartment and, as a gift for Betsey, sewed up a little black dress, onto which I sewed on a pink ribbon and, in silver, screened the text: "what would you give for a great pair of tits?"

I get to the party. The place is packed with people drinking champagne and shoveling chocolate-covered strawberries into their mouths, and Betsey Johnson is standing by the door, tan and lovely, in a shirt that says: "Guys Love B.J."

I loathe doing things like this, but since I'm already there, I figure I may as well swallow my pride and risk sounding like a complete asshole. I approach her and go, hi, I'm Periel, you bought my shirt earlier today, and um, I made you something.

I felt like a complete asshole, but obviously, it was much too late to turn back, so I pulled out the dress and gave it to Betsey Johnson.

She screamed, you're a creative genius!

An editor at a fashion trade newspaper who had been privy to all this screaming ran a piece that called me a fledgling designer.

And thus began my foray into the fashion world. And my foray into the fashion world coincided with my foray into the Church of Latter-day Saints.

It happened like this: Kat and I were in a supermarket and I noticed she was buying a box of herbal chai.

I was like, Kat, what are you doing?

And she was like, what do you mean, what am I doing?

And I was like, what do you mean, what do I mean? I mean, what are you doing? Why are you buying herbal chai? Since when do you drink that shit?

She goes, it's for book club.

I was like, excuse me? Book club? Is that like Breakfast Club? As it turns out, book club is not at all like Breakfast Club. As it turns out, book club is when Kat's friends from the cult come over and they discuss, well, books. Or more precisely, one book.

I go, o-kay.

And Kat goes, what's wrong with book club?

I was like, nothing. Nothing's wrong with book club, I just don't understand why you're buying herbal chai like a fucking Hare Krishna instead of coffee like a normal person.

And so Kat goes, no coffee, no tea. It's against the health code, it's against the Word of Wisdom.

I should mention here that Kat slugs back coffee and martinis like nobody's business. I should also mention that while caffeine and alcohol are strictly forbidden, Mormons have absolutely no qualms about consuming obscene amounts of sugar, mostly in the form of baked goods like lemon squares and "Mormon punch," which consists of a block of rainbow sherbet and a two-liter bottle of Sprite. One sip is, essentially, the equivalent of three lines of crystal meth.

That's right, I say, I forgot. These people are freaks, you understand. I was like, you understand that, right?

Kat: They're not freaks.

Me: They are freaks. They are so freaks.

Kat: You shouldn't be so judgmental. You haven't even met them. You should at least see for yourself.

Me: What do you mean, meet them? You want me to come to book club?

Kat: No, I want you to come to church.

Me: That's very funny. I could really see myself in a Mormon church. I'm sure I would fit in very well.

Kat: I'm serious. You should come.

Slowly I go, Kat, there is not a chance in hell—wait, let me reiterate that—not a chance in hell that I am going to Mormon church.

Cut to: Sunday afternoon, and I'm in a taxi on my way to Mormon church.

I'm like, Kat, you know what I think? I think that you've spent this whole summer snuggling up next to me just so you could try to convert me to Mormonism.

Kat responds to this by ignoring me. She goes, my sister is driving me crazy. She's grumpy all the time, and every time I have book club or have someone over, she gets vicious and gives me the silent treatment.

I was like, well, maybe you should stop having book club.

Kat goes, I'm serious, Periel. I don't know what to do. It's gotten really bad, and the only thing I can think of doing is what I did when I was on my mission—Kat was like, Periel, what are you doing?

I had crawled all the way to a corner of the back of the cab and kind of stuffed myself between the front and back seats.

Again Kat was like, Periel, what are you doing?

I crawled back up into the seat and was covering my face with my bag. I was like, I'm hiding. I was like, I'm hiding because you just said "when I was on my mission."

Kat shot me a filthy look.

I was like, I'm just kidding, go on.

She was like, no, now I'm not going to tell you.

And I was like, will you please get on with it?

She gave me another dirty look and then continued: When I was on my mission, they told us that if we didn't like our companion or if our companion was doing something that we couldn't stand on a regular basis or whatever [I don't know how these things work; I guess when you go on a Mormon mission, you're paired up with someone], then we should serve them.

I'm not kidding. That's what she said.

Serve them?

Yes, Kat said. Serve them. Like make their bed, bring them dinner, that sort of thing.

I offered: Kill them with kindness?

Kat ignored the fact that I said "kill them with kindness" because she knew I was saying "kill them with kindness" in a very tongue-in-cheek sort of way, and so she was like, yes, serve them. It builds empathy and healing.

I was like, how about actually talking about what the fuck is going on? How about instead of baking them a goddamn tuna casserole, or whatever it is that Mormons eat, you do what you really want to do and fling tuna casserole in their fucking face? This is such typical Gentile nonconfrontation.

And Kat was like, that's pretty aggressive, Periel.

And I was like, you know what, fair enough. I was like, you know what, I can understand that making someone's bed might make them feel better.

And Kat was like, it does. It really does.

And I was like, well, maybe it does.

After all, I really can be quite reasonable. I can admit that being nice to someone who is being an asshole might be helpful, because if someone is being an asshole, then most likely that person is suffering. I mean, miserable people behave miserably for a reason. I acknowledged this. However, I continued, the fact of the matter is that while in the short term making someone's bed might be helpful, in the long term you haven't really solved anything. In the long term, you still have to deal with what's going on.

Kat was like, uh.

Uh, as in, I know and you're right. Uh, as in, you're right and this sucks.

I was like, look, I'll tell you a little trick. I'll tell you a trick I learned in a communication class when I was in college. I was like, you want to know?

And Kat was like, yes, yes, tell me.

I was like, look, this is a trick, okay? And it's kind of a secret, so don't go around telling all the Mormons about it. The way to confront someone in a situation such as this is to employ the positive, negative, positive. In this case, with your sister, for example, you would be like, look, I know that you've been under a lot of stress lately and you've been working really hard, and I really admire you, I really admire what you've been doing, I know that it's been very difficult for you, and I think what you're doing is amazing, but I have to tell you, it's been sort of dreadful to talk to you lately. And then you end with something positive.

Kat was like, that's really good, Periel, that was really, really good.

And I was like, oh yeah? Good. I'm glad you liked it.

And I guess that's why I could never hate Kat. Because in spite of it all, she's very reasonable. While she has certainly latched on to some pretty far-fetched, *un*-reasonable ideas, if you present her with a cogent argument as to why a certain theory or idea is absurd, she's very open-minded. It follows, then, that she is amenable to not being attached to something just for the sake of being attached to it, which is a quality I consider critical. Being committed to something simply because you are or because you've been told to be is moronic. It's moronic and it's also indicative of many things, none of them good. Ignorance may be bliss, but it also makes people monstrous.

Kat isn't like this. After all, she did get disfellow-shipped. What does that mean? It means the little fucker got put on probation. Why did she get put on probation? Because she was engaging in sexual behavior. She was engaging in sexual behavior, and she felt very guilty about this because she had been brainwashed by the Latter-day Saints to think that engaging in sexual behavior was sinful. In short, she got fingered and told the bishop. And he disfellowshipped her. Which is like being put on probation, and in the whole Mormon scheme of things, it's really a big deal. It's very serious, because being put on probation is only one step away from being excommunicated entirely. But instead of checking in with a probation officer, Kat had to go see the bishop every week.

I'm not kidding.

For my part, I'm nearly certain that all this cavorting and speaking of sexual matters in closed quarters with Kat gave the bishop a raging hard-on. The bishop, incidentally, is just some dude. I'm dead fucking serious about that. In the Mormon Church, the bishop just, like, becomes a bishop. There's no training or anything. He's literally just some guy from the community who decides he wants to be bishop. Then he's bishop. All you need to do to become a bishop is have a cock.

This particular bishop who disfellowshipped Kat was a businessman. When she told me this, I was like, Kat, I am begging you to tell me you're kidding. Tell me he wasn't really a businessman.

Kat was like, I'm not kidding. Well, I don't know if he was or he wasn't, this was a long time ago. He was that type anyway. He looked like a corporate guy.

Me: And this is normal?

Kat: Yes, it's normal. He's the one you're supposed to

talk to if you have a problem, including if you want to make a confession. He's a spiritual advisor.

Me: ACCORDING TO WHAT? WHY? HOW THE FUCK IS THIS GUY QUALIFIED? BUSINESSMEN ARE THE SLEAZIEST PEOPLE ON EARTH!

Kat: You're crazy, Periel.

Me: *I'm* crazy? Can women become bishops?

Kat: No.

Me: No?

Kat: Of course not.

Me: Of course not? This is reasonable?

Kat: To become bishop, you have to hold the priesthood.

Me: And how does one, shall we say, "hold the priesthood"?

Kat: It gets passed to you.

Me: From whom?

Kat (perturbed): From someone who has it.

Me: What is this, pass the fucking flag? This is like a sexually transmitted disease.

Kat: It gets passed to you. Jesus gave it to his apostles and so on.

I can't believe that even after that crazy conversation,

Kat still managed to persuade me to go to church with her. I don't know how or why I even engage this lunacy, this fucking Mormon lunacy, but I do, and my curiosity landed me smack in the middle of the chapel of the Latter-day Saints. And for what it's worth, this session at church wasn't just any old session. This session at church was on the first Sunday of the month, which is when something called "fast and testimony" takes place. This whole ordeal was so unbelievable that it rendered me almost speechless.

Fast and testimony is when people go up to the pulpit and "bear their testimony." This basically entails having people talk about how they *know* that Joseph Smith is a prophet, how they *know* the Church is true, and finally, about how they *know* God loves them. "Outlandish" would be a good way to describe it, if it weren't such an understatement. It quickly became very clear to me that these people were bugging out.

Having never been to Mormon church before, I was also bugging out. The whole religion is really very out there. Very, very out there. And it's not that other religions aren't out there, but the problem with Mormonism is that there's no wiggle room. It's all or nothing. Which,

74

I suppose, is necessary in order to keep people like sheep that are easy to herd.

Anyway, all these people were getting up there and "bearing their testimonies." Meanwhile, I'm sitting there with my mouth open so wide someone could have shoved a cactus into it and I probably wouldn't have noticed. All these people are getting up there and talking about how happy they are, and seriously, moments after saying that, they start bawling.

The first person to bear testimony waddles over to center stage. She is very short, with eyes that are too close together and curly cropped black hair. She goes, I just wanted to say that I'm really, really grateful for the Lord and how He knows me and knows what I need. Until I invited the Lord into my life, I felt like I was on a big sailboat out in the middle of the ocean all by myself. I know the Book of Mormon is true.

I look at Kat.

She smiles.

I take notes. One would think that people would notice that there is a small Jew in the room furiously scribbling in her notebook, but everyone is so fucking mesmerized that no one does.

The next testimony is similar to the first: I know Joseph Smith is a prophet and I know that Jesus Christ died for our sins. I don't know what to say except that everyone keeps coming up to me and telling me that I look so happy. And I am. And then she starts sniveling.

Most disturbing is the young man who recounts his conversion. Apparently, this guy's mother had died, and come Mother's Day, he was all alone in his apartment, beside himself with grief, when the missionaries knocked on his door. They "saved" him, and in exchange for having been saved, I suppose, he now donates ten percent of his yearly income to the church. I'm sure he'll be very happy when he gets to the VIP room in the celestial level of heaven and they tell him they're filled to capacity.

Next up for fast and testimony is a girl with dishwater-colored hair: This is the first time I'm bearing my testimony, and I know without a doubt that the temple is the only peaceful place on earth. Dishwater Hair breaks down and begins to sob uncontrollably: I just (sob) want to say that I (sob) love my family.

And then the guy who's soon to be a missionary: I am so grateful for my father in heaven. I have so much gratitude, and I know He must love me so much. I know for a fact that Joseph Smith was a prophet. I just want to say that I am going on my mission and that our work is exploding. Our missionary work is spreading like wildfire. The Lord is watching over you. I am so excited to see this work progress.

Then—and this was the best: A blonde number steps up to the fucking pulpit and goes, I promised myself I was not going to cry. And then she starts crying. Then she starts going on about how when she was in first grade, her teacher was mean to her.

I was in shock now. I could not believe what was going on here. The whole thing was just, like, so fucking self-indulgent. These people needed therapy, not church.

Then, or maybe it was before all this testimony shit, they handed out croutons. Or whatever—wafers, bits of bread. Kat turned hers down, but I accepted mine. She gave me a filthy look and whispered, that's the body of Christ.

I popped it into my mouth and was like, so what? I'm hungry.

When we got outside, I was like, girl, you have a good deal of explaining to do.

Kat goes: There's nothing to explain.

Oh, really? You just took me to a cult meeting and you

think there's nothing to explain? You just took me to a room where people were singing things like, "Lean on my ample arm, I'm a pilgrim," and you think you have nothing to explain? Are you out of your fucking mind?

And when we talk about these things and I use words like "indoctrination" and "brainwashed," Kat says I fall short because I just assume it's impossible for someone to have actually thought critically about such things and still arrive at this way of life. Or this way of thinking. Or this religion—or whatever the fuck you want to call it. But it's not so much that. It's that the very thing that makes organized religion so insidious is that *fundamentally*, it is crucial that you *don't* think critically about the tenets of said religion. It becomes a matter of "faith." That's the whole fucking point of religion. And the fucking problem. And it *is* indoctrination.

I started wondering whether Kat's whole Mormon thing was more of a cultural than a religious thing. I don't know. It's all very bizarre. She goes to these Mormon functions, but she never really has a good time. She never actually enjoys the company. And then she goes out on all these "dates" with Mormon guys. I've met several of them, and they're all fucking gay. As in homosexual. Each and every last one of them is a homosexual. And even though I agree with Gore Vidal when he says that there is no such thing as a homosexual or a heterosexual, that there are simply homosexual and heterosexual acts, every single time she has introduced me to some guy from church in whom she is interested or who is interested in her, he's been gay.

How do I know? Because I know. That's fucking how. For the same reason that if you met me and I told you that I'm a Jew or that I have fucked girls or have snorted cocaine, you wouldn't be all that surprised. Because if you're from a particular cultural sphere, these things are not all that difficult to discern.

And the thing is, it makes you wonder—and I have voiced this to Kat—whether there is a reason she is attracting all the gays. What is it that makes all the gay Mormons flock to her? I'm not really sure. Except that the homosexualists, as Vidal calls them, us, whatever, are usually pretty keen in detecting who is and who is not a homophobe. Either that or they like her outfits. Maybe a combination of the two. You see, being gay and Mormon is like being, well, I don't know what it's like, but it's not okay with the Church. Which, as I've pointed out, is one of the problems with Mormonism—no wiggle room.

But some people, like Kat, enjoy certain things about being Mormon. They're just not fundamentalists. And the Mormon Church really screws itself here. The Mormon Church, in all its corrupt glory, winds up losing lots of customers and lots of tithes.

The Jews, who are much more business-savvy than the Gentiles, picked up on this early and were like, well, if everyone has to walk around with big black hats and curly pubes hanging off the sides of their heads, we're going to lose all our people. So they were like, fuck it, what do we care, you can wear whatever you want, and some of you will be the "real" Jews but the rest of you can still be Jews. The real Jews will wear the outfits and won't really consider the rest of you Jews, but it won't matter. The rest of you can still go set up temples and celebrate holidays, and be gay, and the real Jews won't think you're Jewish, but you won't care about that anyway, and as long as you donate money to the synagogue, neither will we.

The Mormons, on the other hand, were not even trying to hear this. You have to be a little bit flexible now and then. I think the Mormon homosexualists are like Kat in that they have grown up in this culture (if eating lemon squares and making scrapbooks can be considered a culture) and they feel comfortable in it. Like Kat, as well, they recognize that most if not all of the other people at church are bugging out.

The best part about going to church with Kat were the two guys sitting to my left. They were sitting very close to each other and one of them had his hand on the other one's back. I took both mental and physical note of this and I was like, hmmm, that's a bit odd. So I nudged Kat to look. She tried to play it off. "Brotherly," I believe, was the word she used.

Then, by about twenty minutes into the sermon, the one guy had moved his hand to the other guy's *knee*. I was like, whoa. I was like, whoa, as in, this could really get good. I nudged Kat again, and there was no denying that she was a bit surprised by this overt act of homosexual behavior right there in the middle of the service at the church of Latter-day Saints. Then the one guy started rubbing the other guy's leg, and the guy who was being rubbed sort of leaned his head onto the shoulder of his "friend."

When we got outside, I could barely contain myself. I was like, did you see that?

And Kat was like, see what?

And I was like, don't bullshit me, Kat, you know

what I'm talking about, those guys were about to start giving each other blowjobs.

And Kat was like, Periel, please, that's absurd.

And I was like, oh, really? It's absurd? You're telling me it's normal for two guys to be sitting in the middle of church massaging each other?

And Kat goes, maybe one of them was really upset. Maybe they were brothers.

I go: Does your brother run his hands up between your legs?

Kat goes: Okay, okay. I admit, it was bizarre.

I say: Incest is the last taboo of our culture.

Kat: What does incest have to do with anything?

Me: Nothing, I'm just saying.

Later, in what was perhaps an attempt to understand the Jews better, Kat started fooling around with a Jewish guy named Jonathan, whom I referred to as Yonatan.

Kat, being a Mormon, and therefore more familiar with the New Testament than the Old, did not know that "Yonatan" is Hebrew for "Jonathan," and so each time I would ask, "What's up with Yonatan?" she would be like, who? And then I'd be like, you understand that if you marry this guy, you're going to have to convert to Judaism, right? I meant it half in jest and half seriously because the fact of the matter is, Kat does want to get married. Ultimately, that's what I want, she says. Ultimately what *I* want, I tell her, is to not die a hideous, painful premature and petrifying death.

I tell her, Kat, you have to understand that no Jewish mother is going to let her son marry a fucking Mormon. I mean, it's just out of the question. What would she tell her friends? Seriously, I love Kat, I do, but being Mormon is fucking weird. And Jewish mothers, for the most part, want their kids to marry other Jews so that they can have Jewish grandchildren. I expressed this to Kat. She said she'd be okay converting to Judaism, since that was her second-favorite religion. I have no idea why this pleased me so much, but it did. We would welcome you with open fucking arms, I told her.

Anyway, Kat met this guy, she liked him, and so, as she is wont to do, she pursued him. And they began to do things together. Like go out, see movies, go to cafés, walk around, and occasionally, sleep over at each other's places.

All the while something being a little off. All the while Kat knowing that this guy was a little bit iffy, a little bit stuffy, a little bit, shall we say, tedious. But Kat, being a Mormon—and this may or may not have anything to do with that, but it is true nonetheless—is always giving people the benefit of the doubt.

Until one day when he slept over at her house and she had just finished being aroused, which means that she was *no longer* aroused, which means that she had just climaxed but was no longer climaxing. In fact, she had wandered off from the place where she had been aroused, where she had climaxed, which was on the couch, and had gone to the kitchen.

And he, Yonatan, who was *still* aroused (and she knew he was still aroused because of the unmistakable outline of an erection poking through the thin material of his boxer shorts), had followed her into the kitchen.

It was at this point that Kat blurted out, I think we should just be friends.

Which is something she had been thinking for a while. She had been thinking this for a while because, like I said, she knew that Yonatan was a little bit dull, a little bit stuffy, with a sort of tedious and dull sense of humor. Simply not for me, as she put it.

At this, Yonatan, with his hard-on, became very angry and said, do you really think this is an appropriate time to discuss this?

And so Kat was like, look, our senses of humor don't really mix.

Which was only one of the things she said, but Yonatan seized on it. He seized on it and basically freaked, because apparently his last girlfriend had dumped him for what amounted to the same reason. And this guy, this fucking guy Yonatan, starts going to Kat, well, *I* think I'm a funny guy. In fact, I think I'm a *damn* funny guy. And I think you're starting to come around to see that too.

Can you imagine having the gall to say something like that? *Especially* to someone who was just nice enough *not* to tell you that your personality sucks. *I think you're starting to come around?*

Kat scrunched up her face and was like, I don't think so, Yonatan.

Though I'm quite certain that she didn't call him Yonatan. And I wasn't there, so I can't say for sure that she scrunched up her face, but I would bet she did, mostly because that's what she always does when she's having a conversation like this. Which is a conversation she has more often than not.

I mean, Kat's a real heartbreaker. Plus, she's always dating guys who are infinitely less interesting than she is, so nothing ever lasts. I keep telling her that with all these problems she has with guys, she should start dating women, and she says she's not into it, except that once I took her to a lesbian bar, and believe me, she *was* into it.

Anyway, to Yonatan she goes, I don't think so.

And Yonatan was like, well, so, what are you saying? Are you saying that you think we need to see more of one another?

Which is really sort of amazing.

And Kat was like, um, no, that's not what I'm saying at all. Actually, I'm saying quite the opposite. I'm saying that we need to see *less* of one another.

And Yonatan, who was apparently a bit baffled by all this, goes, well, where do you see us in the future?

And Kat was like, what do you mean, where do I see us in the future?

And Yonatan was like, well, what's your vision of us? Where do you see us?

And Kat, who at this point must have been even more baffled than Yonatan—like, *how is this guy so fucking dense?*—said, I see us frolicking in a meadow.

Yonatan didn't think that was very funny.

But I do. I think that's fucking funny as shit. I think it's fucking hilarious. And when Kat told me the story, it was obvious that she did as well. But Yonatan didn't. He never did. Poor Yonatan never recognized the humor in this. He never recognized that, really, "I see us frolicking in a meadow" was a brilliant thing to say.

Which is exactly why she had to get rid of him. Or at least one of the reasons. Because that wasn't the sort of thing Yonatan thought was funny. The sort of thing Yonatan thought was funny, according to Kat, was when the two of them would be walking down the street and would pass a parking lot that had a big sign that read "Park," and Yonatan would sort of chortle and go, wow, that guy Park sure owns a lot of real estate, huh?

And then he would pause.

And look at Kat, waiting for, I don't know, waiting for something.

And then, when Kat wouldn't laugh, he would go, that was a joke.

Kat says he would do that sort of thing all the time. He would say something that was in no way clever or funny and then look at her like he had just offered her some sort of gem.

One night Kat and Yonatan were walking in her neighborhood on the Upper West Side of Manhattan, and Yonatan was scared. Kat lives up on Central Park West. Sort of Harlem, but not really. More Upper West Side than Harlem. My point is that this is *not* a dangerous neighborhood. But they were walking past this group of thug guys. And one of them was looking at Yonatan. One of these thug guys was clocking him, and this guy had one marble eye. And as he was clocking Yonatan with his one not-marble eye and his one marble eye, Yonatan goes, good evening.

Good evening?

Who the fuck says good evening to a thug with a marble eye?

Someone with no fucking intuition, that's who.

Along these same lines, there was the time that Kat's car got broken into and apparently there was some sketchy character who had been sort of lurking around near the car before it got broken into. So when the cops get there, they start asking questions, like whether either Kat or Yonatan saw anything questionable.

And Yonatan goes, well, there was an African-American gentleman. . . .

And the cop was like, well, he couldn't have been that much of a gentleman if he broke into your car.

Ad fucking nauseam. All of these things were connected, all of these little incidents, which alone indicated all sorts of things, you could add them up. And when you added them up, what you came up with was the unequivocal fact that Jonathan was just not that cool. Not that interesting. Not that inspired. Not that *anything*.

And this was in large part why Kat had to rid herself of this guy, though I am willing to concede that perhaps she shouldn't have broken the news while he still had an erection.

For her part, Kat maintains that this was the *best* time to break the news.

When I inquired as to why, she scrunched up her face and said, because I knew I had his full attention.

One of the reasons that Kat could never entirely hand herself over to Mormonism is that she is an egomaniac.

This is not a criticism. In fact, it's something I appreciate a good deal. If she weren't an egomaniac, she'd never have done what she did and I would never have gotten the idea to do what I did. By that I mean: I gave Kat a "the only bush I trust is my own" tank top. In turn, she gave me a photo. A rather provocative shot of her in her underwear and the tank top, motioning downward toward, well, her bush. I was, let's say, turned on. Not in an I-want-to-fuck-Kat kind of way—that window, as we know, had closed with the Book of Mormon cutting into my ass—but more in a this-could-be-something kind of way. With Kat's photo taped to the wall above my desk for inspiration, I started sending shirts to friends, asking them to send me photos of themselves.

I thought I would do something like that Alfredo Jaar "Rwanda" poster that Brooke Fenster-Bloom had ripped off, something Barbara Kruger/Guerrilla Girls–esque. It would be like a visual protest piece for the 2004 presidential election, a poster called "100 Reasons Not to Vote for Bush" with one hundred photos of women in the tank top, with each woman's name, age, and occupation accompanying her photo. Obviously, I would need to round up the one hundred photos of one hundred women, but how hard could that be?

In theory, it would be very simple. In practice, it was a pain in the fucking ass. You would think I was asking people to slice off their nipples and mail them to me on ice. It's a big hassle, apparently, to have your photo taken and mail or e-mail it to someone.

The real hassle was that most women wanted to look pretty, and so there was the whole routine of having to put on makeup and do their hair. Then, inevitably, they would think they looked fat and have to go through the whole fucking process again. And while I can certainly relate to such shallowness, I nevertheless got totally fed up. So I did what any guerrilla would do. I took to the streets.

I had a friend take me to a peep-show parlor he frequents to jerk off and watch girls shove vibrating plastic camels up their asses. The girls were up for being photographed in the tank top, but none of them would agree to being identified in the poster as a peep-show girl. I was like, look, I'm trying to get a representative sample of women, and the fact that you're a librarian when you're not shoving plastic animals up your ass is great, but I already have a photo of a librarian. One of them finally acquiesced.

The best track, I found, was to wear the tank top

whenever I went out anywhere. That was number one. Number two was to have my camera and a substantial number of shirts in my bag. Then all I had to do was linger around women who looked like good subjects until they commented on the shirt (like, I love that shirt). After that, it was simply a question of moving in for the kill. I would explain the project, and if they were into it, which most of them were, I would then usher them into the nearest bathroom for wardrobe change and photo shoot.

There was only one recurring problem. I was screening people and, in so doing, carefully selecting women who stood out in some way. But many of the women I wanted to photograph were inevitably saddled with friends who also wanted to have their photographs taken, and it was impossible to turn down the friends. I wound up giving away many, many shirts.

Then, from out of nowhere, the list arrived. A friend of a friend had gotten wind of what I was doing and had sent me a huge list with the home addresses of everyone from Sandra Bernhard to, like, the Princess of Jordan. I wondered if the Princess of Jordan would send me a photograph of herself in a tank top that read "the only bush i trust is my own." My guess was no. I continued perusing. And then I saw it.

Susan Sarandon. Now in all fairness, I have to say that because I don't have a television or go to the movies, I am, for the most part, unfamiliar with Susan Sarandon's work as an actress. In the early nineties, I saw a film called *White Palace* and adored her in that, but I knew her mostly because I had seen her speak at an antiwar rally in Central Park.

I admired Susan Sarandon because she had the balls to say what many other celebrities were thinking but wouldn't say, for fear it would hurt their career. I admired Susan Sarandon because she was more interested in speaking out than in worrying about whether or not she would be offered a $19 billion contract to endorse Coca-Cola. While I very much liked her as an actress, I *loved* her as an activist. So when I saw her address on my newly (and very questionably) acquired list, I thought, *yes*. Actually, I thought, maybe. So I fired off a letter explaining who I was and what I was doing and how I wasn't a fashion designer but . . . the whole spiel. I folded the letter and put it into an envelope with a tank top and tried to forget about the whole thing.

Two weeks later, my phone rang.

Hi, I'm calling from Susan Sarandon's office, and we were wondering if this poster you're making is going to be for sale.

I was like, what? Yes. I mean no. No, it's not going to be for sale. Then there was silence.

I was like, hello?

Then: Yes, yes, I'm here. Okay, thank you very much, we'll be in touch.

What did that mean? Was she in or was she out? How would we be in touch? I couldn't believe the shirt had actually gotten there.

I was encouraged by this small step forward. I consulted the list of addresses again and promptly sent a shirt to Madonna. And Sarah Jessica Parker. And Lili Taylor. And well, you get the idea.

Eve Ensler, playwright of *The Vagina Monologues* and, as such, arguably the most famous bush in the United States, invited me to her house to photograph her. Then Gloria Steinem let me know that she was amenable but wouldn't be available for a couple of weeks and didn't want to hold me up. I told her that, all things considered, I thought she was worth waiting for.

I eventually showed up at her door with two bouquets of flowers and took many photos.

This is not to say that everything went smoothly. I sent Sandra Bernhard a shirt and never heard back. This surprised me. She was the one person I actually expected to hear from. Not only did she not even take three seconds to write me a note saying thanks but no, thanks, but she actually wore the shirt on television without even so much as acknowledging the project. The nerve of this woman was shocking. Now, I know Sandra Bernhard's probably a busy person, but as far as I am concerned, that's a fucking crock of shit. Like Susan Sarandon isn't busy? Like *I'm* not fucking busy?

Then there was my eighty-six-year-old grandmother, who let me take a photo of her in the shirt only to tell me a week later that she didn't want me to use it in the poster because she feared her doctors would see it and "think less" of her. I was like, Grandma, I'm so sure your doctors are going to see the poster, but she said she couldn't take the risk.

And then, of course, there was my twenty-one-year-old cousin, who was concerned about future job pros-

95

pects in the corporate world, where she aspires to be gainfully employed once she graduates from college.

I took all of these rejections very personally and will carry with me small grudges against these people for the rest of my natural life. I don't ask people to do things for me very often, but when I do, I expect an enthusiastic, "Yes, I'd love to!" Failing to respond in this fashion not only irritates me but makes me question said person's allegiances as well.

Once I had all my photographs, I was ready to put the poster together. There was just one person left whom I needed. The last person I needed—really needed—to make this complete was my mother.

I called her. Mommy, will you send me a picture of yourself for the poster?

My mother: What? Me?

Me: Yes, you. I have to have you, it won't be the same if you're not in it.

My mother: Now you're asking me to do this?

Me: As opposed to when?

My mother: You were going to take a picture of me last time you came over, and you didn't bring your camera because you're so disorganized.

Me: I'm not disorganized.

My mother: You are disorganized, if you weren't disorganized, you'd already have a picture of me. Everything with you is last-minute.

Me: Whatever. Will you do it or not?

My mother: Do I have a choice?

Me: What do you mean, do you have a choice? Of course you have a choice. Actually, you don't have a choice. But you'll be in good company—Susan Sarandon sent me a photo.

My mother: Yes, I know. I really can't believe that.

Me: What do you mean? Why can't you believe that?

My mother: Because Susan Sarandon is a very sophisticated person, and the language on this shirt, well, let's just say, if you weren't my daughter . . .

Me: Okay, whatever, just get me the photo, I need it, like, yesterday.

My mother: Okay, okay. I really can't believe how you leave things for the last minute. You're very disorganized.

Me: First of all, I happen to be highly organized, and second of all, I have to get off the phone.

My mother: And as usual, you have to go. You're always in a rush. I never get to talk to you.

I hang up. Mari is perched next to me and has already begun to scale the photos to size. She has figured out how to fit five lines of twenty photos that are all exactly the same size and also equidistant from one another on a poster that measures twenty by thirty-six inches. She is putting things together from scratch. I don't understand any of this.

It's amazing to be able to work with someone like this. I had this specific idea in my head for months, but my ignorance prevented me from turning it into anything beyond an idea. Mari gets her hands on it, and within a few hours she is printing out a mock-up that looks exactly like what I had envisioned. A week or so later, as soon as the posters are back from the printer, I start plastering them all over the United States, or at least try to.

I get a website up and running, or, correction, I get someone else to get a website up and running, and suddenly I'm getting orders for this fucking shirt from Texas to Norway. Texas? Yes, Texas.

Because I am filling orders for thousands of shirts, I no longer print the shirts myself. I am running a business, which is absolutely fascinating because I have absolutely no idea how to run a business. I have never taken a business class in my entire life. I can barely add.

The point is that I succeeded, at least on some level, in bucking the system I had railed against at the Little Ivy. I had founded body as billboard: advertise for shit that matters, a sweatshop-free original-artwork clothing line for women sick of companies' appropriation of their bodies for advertising.

I appoint my father secretary-treasurer. All monies coming in or going out pass through him. This is a very good arrangement since my father is meticulous and I am, well, a writer. The fact that I am a writer keeps getting lost in a pile of tank tops, but women keep sending me e-mails and orders that make it all seem worthwhile. It has become eminently clear that I am on a mission to change things—one pair of tits at a time.

In addition to the wonderful e-mails that say things like, "Your words have spread farther than you know. Thank you for representing a sea of women who are no longer asleep," there are, of course, less favorable e-mails to contend with. Like one signed "well-fed and fed-up," berating me for calling myself a feminist while not carrying triple-extra-large "only bush" shirts.

I was like, Dear Well-Fed and Fed-Up, I don't know what to tell you except that I cater to demand, and while I would be more than happy to print you up a custom shirt, I simply don't get enough requests for shirts in that size to warrant keeping them in stock. I mean, this isn't the Gap, you know?

She wrote me back an even more vitriolic reply, basically being like, yeah, whatever, if girls my size don't buy clothes, then why aren't there a bunch of fat naked chicks running around? I don't know why there aren't a bunch of fat naked chicks running around. But like an idiot, I printed up a bunch of gargantuan shirts and received precisely two additional orders. This means that I am now stuck with approximately fifty enormous shirts.

And it's too bad that these enormous shirts weren't *pro*-Bush instead of anti-Bush, because I could have made a killing when the Republican National Convention rolled into town like a goddamned circus in August 2004. New York City was stuffed full of fat Republican women who would have been perfect fits for the leftover stockpile of XXXL tanks.

My first interaction with them was at the "Faith, Family and Freedom" rally, held at the Waldorf-Astoria Hotel, which my editor snuck me into and where they were handing out big blue pins with pictures of fetuses on them and using phrases like "baby killer" and "yeehaw." These women were dressed in red, white, and blue sweaters made of a stringy synthetic material that looked not unlike pubic hair. Before this great nation can truly move ahead, someone needs to explain to the Republican women of America that our flag is not a fashion accessory and should not be used as one.

The day after the family rally, I suited up for an anti-Bush rally with one of my tank tops and my custom-made "Fuck Bush" necklace, which I was relieved had not set off the metal detector while I was on my way into that Republican rally. It was like ninety-seven degrees out, and while I was battling heatstroke and dehydration with Kat, I imagined all the piggish Republicans stretched out in their air-conditioned hotel rooms. On top of that, I have to contend with my mother, who won't stop calling me. At one point I see that I have missed thirteen calls. I finally call her back. Is everything okay? I bellow into the phone.

My mother: Oh, thank god, I was so worried about you. I thought you'd been arrested.

Me: Why would I have been arrested?

My mother: Are you provoking people?

Me: Mommy, please.

My mother: Don't provoke the police officers.

Me: I'm making friends with the police officers. They like me and they like my shirt. I even gave them a few to pass on to their girlfriends and wives. You should be more concerned that I don't get heatstroke. It's, like, four hundred degrees out and I've stripped down to my "only bush" underwear.

My mother: Oh my god. Please be careful. You have to be careful. You have to be careful, otherwise you'll wind up in jail, where you could get physically hurt by drug addicts who are insane, by crack addicts who would see you as bait. I've read about people who were put in jail and then accosted by inmates.

I'm like, look, Mommy, this is ridiculous. I have to go. I'll call you later.

My mother screams, PLEASE BE CAREFUL! Try very hard not to get arrested. That's all I ask.

part two

big balls

My mother, my father, and I were in the car—my father's car—which, like everything else he owns, is immaculate. My father spent several years in the military and it left him with a great fondness for law and order and things of this nature. I think it also left him with borderline obsessive-compulsive disorder. He's not only fanatical about his car, but also about his computer, his cell phone, the VCR, TV, the answering machine, and the dog. You can't touch anything or move anything without him having a nervous breakdown. My father, as it turns out, has a great affinity for things that don't talk, which likely has something to do with the fact that my mother has been chewing his ear off for thirty-some-odd years.

In addition to being immaculate, my father's car is covered in NYPD and FDNY decals and bumper ornaments, and he has a perfectly folded new American flag in the back window, which proves that you don't have to be a fucking asshole Republican to be patriotic. My father is very liberal *and* very patriotic. And while I imagine that he would like nothing more than to support our "commander in chief," he thinks George Bush is a fucking idiot, though he would never say it in quite those terms.

I was like, Pa, if you're going to have an American flag in the back of the car, you could at least get a vintage one. That one looks tacky.

He ignored me. He ignored me and he gave me a dirty look. The dirty look is kind of a signature of his, and giving it is one of his many traits I've inherited. It translates to: *Don't waste my time with bullshit.* My father doesn't like to talk about things, he likes to get them done. I respect this. For example, he had a moustache for most of my life, and then one day, after my mother had been telling him over and over again that he looked like a schnauzer because his hair was still black and his moustache was gray, he shaved it off. He had that thing for like twenty-five years but he never even said a word about getting rid of it. He just walked into the bathroom one day, and when he came out, it was gone.

So when I found an old American flag with forty-eight stars at some army-navy thrift store, I bought it. Although he didn't say a word, I knew he was pleased with it, because he went right ahead and replaced the tacky one with my more stylish edition.

So we're in the forty-eight-star-American-flag car, and I start talking about my friend Cara, whom I've known since we were toddlers growing up in Rego Park, Queens. Our families used to go to the beach club together on weekends—our mothers would sunbathe, our fathers would play paddleball, and she and I would get into all sorts of trouble.

Rego Park is among the most ethnically diverse neighborhoods in New York and therefore in the United States—it's something of a haven for people from all over the world, kind of like a mini–United Nations. It is also kind of, well, ghetto. Like, Cara and I grew up drinking forties and smoking blunts in the park, and many of my friends from high school are in jail or dead. Well, that's not entirely accurate. Many of them are alive and well and dealing drugs.

In any event, Cara and I grew up down the street from each other, and because we grew up down the street from each other, and because we're both only children, and because I'm two years older and a little bit less conventional, our relationship has always been more big-sister, little-sister than friends. I love Cara, but she is actually more like an annoying little sister than a friend. Which is funny, because I am small and my body is kind of boyish and she is tall and her body is, shall we say, curvaceous.

Cara is obsessed with eating, sleeping, and online dating. Online Jewish dating. She's constantly talking about it, and she's formed all these relationships with all these people she's met online. The level that this girl has taken online dating to is so shameless that, quite frankly, I'm compelled by it. I'm compelled by it in the same way one is compelled to look at a car wreck. It's, like, you don't want to be in the car, obviously, and you don't really want something hideous to have happened, but if something hideous did happen, you certainly don't want to miss it.

I think online dating is fucked. I think there is way too much room for error, and I'm much too paranoid to meet someone that way. When you don't trust anyone, the last thing you're going to want to do is meet some freak on the Internet. Maybe I've read too many true-crime books, but nevertheless, that's what I think. Plus, I always think people are lying. Which they are. Kat has met people online who she claims looked "very cute" in their Internet photos, and then she meets them in person and they're like four feet tall and wearing sandals with black knee socks. No, thank you.

I'm not going to lie, though. I have spent a good deal of time surfing online dating sites. There is some weird shit going on out there, let me tell you. Of particular interest to me is a service called craigslist, which was started in San Francisco by a guy named Craig who basically wanted to help people and let them know about cool events in town. It has since turned into a site that spans the globe. There is now even a craigslist Bangalore. You can get anything from a used TV to a blowjob. Which was kind of my own craigslist trajectory. I began by perusing the used-furniture section, where I bought this beautiful colossal old desk from the 1950s. Then I came across what has since become my favorite section of craigslist, the "men seeking men" personals. It's raw and uncensored and, as it turns out, extremely addictive.

For example, one guy was interested in having a

group of guys come over and strap a funnel to his face in order to facilitate "dumping their loads" into his mouth. Another was looking to be strapped facedown on a motel bed for an "anonymous gang bang." And a self-described "cum pig" in Chelsea was bragging about a sling. A sling?

Cara's online dating life is a far cry from the "men seeking men" on craigslist, but I'm compelled by it nonetheless. Mainly because I have to hear about it all the time. The way I see it is that if I have to hear about it all the time, I may as well conjure up some way to be compelled by it. So now I'm compelled. These dating services are Jewish dating services, so Cara is meeting all these guys who are supposedly straight Jewish men, and the whole deal is kind of like a postmodern version of the ancient tradition of matchmaking except that you make your own match and you do so by logging on to a Jewish website.

This is my understanding of how the thing works: You put your picture online and create a profile. You describe yourself. You talk about what you like, what you don't like, what you're looking for in a mate. The dating service gives you the beginning of the sentence and you fill in the blanks.

Cara's profile looks something like this: I am a neurotic Jewish princess, LA transplant from NY, I'm a graduate student, my favorite food is sushi, I'm a dog person, and my annual income is undisclosed. One thing I can tell you for goddamn sure is that her annual income is undisclosed because it doesn't exist.

The "perfect match" portion of her profile reads as follows: "A great sense of humor is very important. My parents, who have been married for thirty-three years, say they have a great marriage because my mom likes dark meat and my dad likes white meat; therefore they can split a chicken very easily. I'd like to share a chicken with a dark-meat man who is sweet, loving, and intelligent, with both a dangerous and a neurotic side. A nice upper body and a puppy wouldn't hurt either."

Cara gets very excited when she gets hits. Getting hits means that men have clicked on to your photograph and read your profile. Cara's always like, I got thirty-seven hits! Can you believe it? I'll be, Car, I just spoke to my agent, I think he might sell my book! And she'll be like, last week I only got twenty-four hits, and this week I got thirty-seven!

Cara couldn't be less interested in the quotidian details of my life. I mean, she loves me and she wants good things to happen to me, but as I said, mostly she's interested in eating, sleeping, and Jewish Internet dating services. When I started making T-shirts, Cara announced that she wanted me to make her a shirt that read, "Will Fuck for Food."

Anyway, through this Jewish Internet dating service, JCupid—which no longer exists, as it has merged with JDate, where there are "hundreds of thousands of member profiles" and "thousands more joining each day"—Cara met this Israeli guy named Tal, who worked as a bodyguard for some actress who has some show I've never heard of because I haven't had a television in, like, twelve years. When things fell apart with Tal, Cara informed me she was going to expand her Jewish online dating life to a different Jewish online dating network, to JDate. This, of course, was before JCupid merged with JDate.

While I was in the car with my parents, I started thinking about a JDate story Cara had told me, about some stockbroker. I would never have thought of it had my mother not been droning on about some "nice Jewish boy." But she was droning on about some nice Jewish boy, which led me to consider telling her this story, in part because I love telling her stories like this, to dispel her idea that Jewish guys are so nice, and also because she thinks that there's nothing wrong with being a stockbroker.

So I was getting all excited at the prospect of telling this story, and then I was like, no, no, I really shouldn't, but then I just couldn't hold back and I was like, fuck it.

So we're in the car, my mother, my father, and I. My father is driving, obviously, because no one drives my father's car except him, and my mother is in the front seat and I'm in the back.

I launch into it:

Cara met this guy, Brian Liebnitz, on the Internet. He's a stockbroker.

My mother: That's nice.

Me: Why is that nice? Being a stockbroker is disgusting.

My mother: Peri, really.

Me: It's outrageous that I say he's a stockbroker and you say, "That's nice." If I said he was a garbageman, you wouldn't have said that.

My mother: Being a garbageman isn't quite as respectable as being a stockbroker.

Me: Cara said he sounded really nice over the phone.

My mother: He does sound very nice.

Me: How does he sound nice? He wasn't nice. The

113

first time she met him, he said that instead of going out, they should stay home and watch television.

My mother: Maybe he wanted to get to know her.

Me: Yeah, he got to know her really well. He jerked off and came all over her leg.

My mother, with her Israeli accent, is going, oh my god, oh my god, how disgusting, I can't believe you're telling me this. Oh my god, who is this person?

And I was like, he's a stockbroker. I thought you said being a stockbroker was respectable. Cara told me that while they were hooking up he started saying things like, rub my big cock.

And my mother goes, OH MY GOD. How awful.

I go, he's a stockbroker. How could a stockbroker do something like that?

And of course my mother says, how do you know he's a stockbroker? Which is exactly what I was saying before, that my mother finds it very difficult to believe that someone as "respectable" as a stockbroker could behave in such a manner. Which is to say too, as I also said before, that I take enormous pleasure in shattering my mother's image of stockbrokers. First it was "very nice" that he's a stockbroker, but now she doesn't believe that he really is one. Typical.

And he's Jewish, I reminded her.

How do you know he's Jewish? He told her that, but how do you know it's true? Oh my god, how disgusting. Peri, please, I really don't want to hear this.

Don't forget about my big balls, I said.

My father was cracking up.

My mother's going, every time I see Cara's parents, this is all I'm going to think about, stop it, really. Oh my god, how disgusting.

Don't forget about my big balls, rub my big balls, I want to come on your big tits, I want to come on your big tits. But Cara wouldn't let him. So instead he came all over her leg, like a dog.

My father was like, why wouldn't she let him?

And my mother's going, Michael, please, don't encourage her. Who behaves like this? How could she do that? How terrible. And then my mother goes, I'm going to tell you something, but you better not write about this. She was like, I'm serious, I'm never going to tell you anything again if you write about this. My mother says this to me all the time. My mother was like, this story is unbelievable. She was like, it's really such a sad story, it's really terrible. Especially since we know Roz, she's from the neighborhood.

I was like, you don't know Roz. I was like, you know Roz because Cara's mother knows Roz.

My mother was like, we *do* know Roz, it's terrible, you better not write about this, no one is supposed to know.

I had already heard this story from Cara but played dumb.

For twenty-some-odd years, Roz (who, for the record, is also Jewish) worked for this elderly woman in Manhattan, and during the course of these twenty years, she stole like three zillion dollars from this woman, and then she got caught, after the woman became too old and moved in with her daughter and her daughter's attorney husband in Connecticut. The daughter found a check signed by her mother and she was like, hmmm.

She was like, hmmm, because it was impossible that the woman had signed anything, because she had become too elderly to sign anything, which was precisely why she had moved in with her daughter in the first place. So the daughter showed this thing to her attorney husband, who was also like, hmmm.

And because of this, the daughter and the husband

became suspicious and confronted Roz, who, on account of all this, landed herself in a women's prison.

My mother was like, this is really a terrible story. My mother was like, we know Roz, we've known Roz for years.

I was like, you do *not* know Roz, you sort of know Roz.

My mother always pulls shit like this. She always tries to say that she knows someone better than she really does, she always makes like she knows people, when really she only sort of knows them. Especially when they're Jewish.

My mother continued, Cara's mother went to visit Roz in jail and it's just horrible. My mother was like, even years ago, we all knew she was stealing, because Roz lived the most lavish lifestyle. She had this enormous house, a mansion really, and she would eat in five-star restaurants, she would take these extravagant vacations, and her husband [whose name, I think, is Ernie, but my dad kept saying it was Bernie to trick me] also got arrested but then they let him go.

And my mother was like, you really can't write about this, my mother was like, I'm serious, no one is supposed to know about this.

I was like, what do you mean, no one is supposed to

know about this? Wasn't this in the papers? I said that because I thought I remembered Cara mentioning something about it being in the papers.

Yes, my mother said, it was in the papers, but anyway, no one is supposed to know, you better not write about it, it's such a terrible story, these people, they're like family.

Family? This incensed me.

I was like, *how* are these people like family?

And my mother was like, they're our people. They're Jews, they're like family.

According to this logic, I said, I suppose that Brian Liebnitz, the stockbroker who ejaculated all over Cara's leg, is also like family.

At this, my mother reconsidered her statement and said, fine. Roz was like a friend and neighbor, even though she wasn't.

And then we stopped to get gas. And I go, Mommy, remember Nadir?

My mother goes, your Arab friend?

Mommy. Nadir's hardly an Arab. He's Pakistani and Pakistanis aren't Arabs.

My mother goes, Pakistanis aren't Arabs? So what are they?

Nadir says they're Semites. Like us. And anyway, he's only *half* Pakistani.

Nadir, for his part, is also known as "Mama." He is twenty-nine years old and looks like Kevin Spacey, but darker and with more hair. He grew up in Alaska and is a classically trained violist, and I met him when I was waitressing at a restaurant in East Harlem. I hated him when I first met him, because I thought he was totally affected—which he is—but then I kind of fell in love with him. He used to run around the restaurant screaming, "Mama has a headache, Mama needs a tranquilizer, a spicy red one." And then he would suck down an enormous Bloody Mary.

Mommy, you know how I went out to dinner with him the other night?

My mother: No, I didn't know. How would I know anything, you never have time to talk to me.

Me: Mommy, that's ridiculous, I talk to you all the time.

My mother: No you don't. Whenever I call you, you never have time, you're always too busy, and anyway, you never tell me anything.

Me: So now I'm telling you something.

My mother: Okay. So what is it?

Me: He told me that he met this guy online and he defecated in the guy's mouth and the guy ate it.

My mother starts screaming, *WHAT?*

My father says nothing.

Me: It's true, Mommy.

My mother: Peri, *please!* What are you talking about?

Me: What do you mean, what am I talking about? Exactly what I'm telling you. Nadir met this guy on the Internet, a Jewish lawyer, mind you, and he defecated in the guy's mouth.

My mother: I don't believe this. I really don't believe this. This is an absolute horror.

Me: What's the big deal? They're two consenting adults.

My mother: This is really terrible.

Me: It's not terrible. It's interesting.

My mother: Enough with the "interesting."

Me: It *is* interesting.

My mother (pauses, then): Oh, no. You're going to write about this, are you?

Me: Of course I am.

My mother: I don't believe this. I really don't believe this. I don't believe you write about things like this. I'm telling you, I absolutely cannot believe this. You're like a college student. You have too much time on your hands to indulge in stupidities.

Me: Oh, come on, Mommy, please. You can't tell me this isn't interesting.

My mother: Here we go again. No, it's not interesting. It's sad. It's very sad that these are the things people are interested in.

Me: Fecal matter?

My mother: Yes. Fecal matter.

Me: Hey, don't knock it till you try it.

My mother: This is awful.

Me: I'm not saying I would do it.

My mother: Well, that's one good thing. I really can't believe people do things like this.

Me: Nadir's a libertine, like Oscar Wilde. He's a little bit depressed.

My mother: Well, maybe if he used a toilet instead of a Jewish lawyer's mouth, he wouldn't be depressed.

Me: Mommy, the guy *wanted* it. It's a sexual thing.

My mother: He *wanted* it? Oh my god. (Pause.) Maybe it's symbolic. Muslims defecating on Jews.

Me: Nadir's hardly Muslim.

My mother: This is sick. This is very, very sick. He's never thought of seeing a psychiatrist? It could be a deficiency. Michael, you don't have anything to say about this?

There's a long pause, and then my father speaks: Is that what turns him on?

Me: I guess so. I mean, obviously.

My mother: It's sick. Michael, you don't think this is sick?

My father: No, Eve, I think it's normal.

My mother ignored this. Of course it's sick. It's very sick. It's the sickest thing I've ever heard. That is really disgusting, I can't believe the people you associate with.

Me: Mommy, I haven't told you the best part yet. Before Nadir went over to meet him, the guy asked him not to eat meat, because he's a vegetarian.

My mother: That's the best part? This is really unbelievable. I don't understand. Isn't he embarrassed?

Me: Why should he be embarrassed?

My mother: No, you're right. He shouldn't be embarrassed. You're right, this is very normal. Really. There's something very wrong with you. I don't want to talk about this anymore.

And that was the end of that.

For as fucked up as most people are with their bodies, I think we *should* talk about these things. Maybe if we talked more, this world wouldn't be in such a state of complete and utter fucking disaster. I mean, maybe if people talked more, human beings wouldn't be committing the *most* fucking dastardly acts against one another. Maybe there would be some fucking chance for this planet to be something other than completely fucking doomed.

Maybe. And I say *maybe* because I'm not a fucking moron. I'm not saying that we should all line up and start shitting in one another's mouths in order to achieve world peace. I'm not saying that at all.

What I *am* saying is that it's important to not have things that are taboo. I mean, at the very least, it's a good place to begin.

After Mama told me his pooing story, I decided to do some investigative reporting. Which is why I went to the bookstore and how I wound up in front of Stan at the information desk.

Stan, who identifies himself as such with a small plastic nameplate over his left nipple that says, "Welcome, my name is: Stan," looks up from his computer and says, can I help you?

I say, yes, I am looking for a book called *History of Shit*.

Stan blanches and twitches and then rifles around on his computer. Then he goes, it's been sent back to the publisher.

I was like, what? why?

Stan, who is unable to hide his pleasure in reporting this, says, because it didn't sell enough copies.

I am disgusted. What kind of world do we live in? What kind of world do we live in when I walk into what is, essentially, the McDonald's of bookstores (I know, I know, I had no business going there to begin with) and I ask an employee a question—a very simple question, mind you—about something every single human being does more or less every single day of his life, and the guy is scandalized. I mean, the guy is fucking scandalized.

Had I asked Stan about a book on date rape or female genital mutilation, he wouldn't have flinched. Had I asked about a book on Phil Knight, the former president of Nike and arguably one of the biggest fucking scumbags on the entire planet, the guy wouldn't have flinched. Meanwhile, the woman in front of me asked him if they had a book called something like *A Carbohydrate Addict's Guide to Eating,* and *that* is normal. They have *A* fucking *Carbohydrate Addict's Guide to Eating* but they don't have *History of Shit*.

Why? Because they sent it back to the publisher. Why did they send it back to the publisher? Because it hadn't sold enough fucking copies. *A Carbohydrate Addict's Guide to Eating,* on the other hand, *has* sold enough copies to warrant being stocked on the third shelf past the mysteries because, apparently, it has sold enough copies to warrant keeping it in the store.

Why? Because people are fucking brainwashed to think that it's more important to be obsessed with carbs than to be interested in something that their own bodies produce, that's fucking why.

Well, I say, do you have anything else?

Stan goes, do I have anything else what?

Do you have any other books?

Any other books?

Any other books *on shit?*

Stan: I don't know, it's not really my area of expertise.

Well, Stan, it's not really *my* fucking area of expertise either, which is why I'm trying to find a fucking book about it. Is *A Carbohydrate Addict's Guide to* fucking *Eating* your area of expertise? You knew where that book was. This is a big problem. This is a big fucking problem, *Stan.* You don't have the fucking book because not enough people are buying the book, and not enough people are buying the book because no one is allowed to talk about shit without everyone having a fucking nervous breakdown.

Why?

Because we're totally repressed. Because we hate our fucking bodies. And we hate our bodies because we're totally detached from them and we're totally detached from them because we're too fucking busy shoving carbs into our faces and becoming obese and reading fucking nonsense by some quack pseudo-nutritionist who is cashing in on the fact that we hate our bodies and are obese, by writing a piece-of-shit book called *A Carbohydrate Addict's Guide to Eating*. No books on shit, but plenty of shitty books.

I turn to walk away, and the woman behind me, who has a blue-tinted beehive and is, like, eighty-six years old, apparently overheard this whole exchange, looks at me, shakes her head, and goes, terrible. Just terrible.

I go, I know, it *is* terrible. Can you believe it? Dominique Laporte is a very respected writer in France. Here, no one even knows who he is.

And the woman narrows her eyes so they become like slits, and hisses and says, no, it's terrible that someone would want to read such filth!

If she hadn't been so old, I would have told her what I thought about her hair. And her breath. But I didn't.

And anyway, you can't really expect someone who was born in, like, 1918 to understand such things. You can, however, expect that Stan would be a bit more fucking helpful. I mean, really.

It's not like Stan doesn't have an anus. It's not like Stan doesn't move his bowels every day. It's not like I'm talking about *this thing that happens to other people*. I'm talking about something that happens to *us*. To all of us. To every single living creature on the face of the earth. We shit. We should talk about this. I am convinced that the anus, together with everything connected to it, is the last taboo of the body. Maybe if we *talked* about this, the gays wouldn't have such a hard time.

I mean, it's a part of life. In certain cases, it's much more a part of life than it should be. For example, the day my bathtub filled up with shit. My landlady is this tiny Japanese woman named Etsuko who speaks fluent, unaccented English when the rent is due, but the day my bathtub starts filling up with shit, suddenly Etsuko doesn't understand a word I am saying.

She comes over and peers into the bathtub and goes,

I see rice. I see the noodle. I see brown food. You no put food in toilet.

And I'm like, Etsuko, I didn't put food in the toilet.

And she goes, you no put pen in toilet, it get stuck. You no flush hambuga meat down toilet!

And then she grabs my sweatshirt and goes, material! material! You put material and food in toilet!

At this point, my apartment completely reeks and I am totally beside myself. So I go, Etsuko, why in the world would I try to flush a sweatshirt down the toilet? That's ridiculous.

And she goes, you put food into toilet, come up into bathtub.

Finally I can't take it anymore, so I go, Etsuko! That's not food in the bathtub! It's feces. Human shit, fecal matter.

And she looks at me as though I have eighteen heads, and goes, this very [but she said "velly"] funny.

Then she busts out this enormous bottle of brown liquid and starts pouring it into the bathtub and into the toilet, and she goes, this velly expensive chemical, velly strong but yes work.

So now the apartment is like burning to the ground

because of this chemical that is wafting through the air, and my eyes feel like someone shot them full of Mace, and I go, well, Etsuko, what are you going to do? I mean, I need to use the bathroom and I'm dirty. I need to take a shower.

And Etsuko goes, you be patient, you use your neighbor bathroom, you shower at neighbor apartment.

So I'm like, Etsuko, I cannot shower at my neighbors' place. I don't even know them. I mean, what do you want me to do? Wrap a towel around myself and knock on my neighbors' door and be like, I know I have never said more than two words to you, because I think you are kind of weird, and actually you freak me out a little bit, but would you mind terribly if I took a shit and showered in your bathroom?

I'm so sure.

The brown chemical eventually did its job, and things cleared up shortly thereafter, and I was soon able to poo in my own toilet again, which is something I very much enjoy doing. Pooing, that is.

I am not embarrassed to talk about this either. As far as I am concerned, pooing is very normal and should not be treated as humiliating. Unless it's like what happened to Cara when she went on one of her weekly JDates. She was particularly excited about this one, and got all decked out to go to some fancy martini bar. The last thing she remembered was that she was prancing around the bar, and the next thing she knew, she was lying in a pile of diarrhea. A cyst had burst on her ovary and she had shit her pants.

When I told this story to my father, the first thing he wanted to know was how she cleaned up. This is always exactly the sort of information my father is most interested in. He is obsessed with cleanliness. I'm surprised he didn't ask how Cara cleaned up after Brian Liebnitz ejaculated on her leg.

Anyway, I am not embarrassed that I have an anus, and am quite pleased with mine. It's very clean and pink, and I think it's quite good-looking. It was, anyway, until the tragedy.

The tragedy was that my anus ballooned to the size of a small child's head. It was, needless to say, not a good scene. But I feel it is important, if not critical, to discuss such things, if for no other reason than to de-stigmatize them. This is my contribution. Think of it as social work.

After I had determined that there was, indeed, something very wrong with my anus, I called my mother at work.

Mommy, I'm having a problem.

My mother: What do you mean, you're having a problem? What kind of a problem are you having?

Me: My ass.

My mother: *What?* Peri, please, what are you talking about?

Me: I'm not kidding. My ass is killing me. I think I have a fissure. I had anal sex and now my ass is seriously killing me.

My mother: OH MY GOD. HOW CAN YOU TELL ME THESE THINGS? I'M AT WORK. THERE'S SOMETHING WRONG WITH YOU. THERE IS SOMETHING SERIOUSLY WRONG WITH YOU. THIS IS WHAT HAPPENS WHEN YOU ABUSE YOUR BODY.

Me: Mommy, will you please calm the fuck down.

My mother, bellowing: LANGUAGE!

Me: I'm not abusing my body. This is perfectly normal. Gay men have anal sex all the time.

My mother: YOU'RE NOT A GAY MAN. And maybe that's why they have so many health problems.

Me: Mommy, really. What should I do?

My mother: This is terrible. This is really terrible. How do you know it's a fissure?

Me: I don't. I just think it is. I called Nadir and that's what he said, because he had one once.

My mother: *That's* who you call? *Someone who defecates in people's mouths?*

Me: Who better?

My mother: I don't know what to tell you except that this isn't natural. It's not a natural thing to do to your body.

Me: Mommy, *please!* People have been having anal sex since the time of the Greeks. You're being ridiculous.

My mother: I'm at work. I can't believe you're telling me these things when I'm at work. You better call your father.

Me: Fine.

I call my father. He answers the phone. I hear Mitch, his paddleball partner, in the background.

I'm like, Pa, I have a problem.

My father: What do you mean, you have a problem?

Me: In my ass. I think I have a fissure.

My father: How did that happen?

Me: I don't know, Pa. How do you think it happened?

My father: I don't know, Peri. If I knew, I wouldn't ask.

Me: Sex.

And then, silence. And then, more silence.

And then, my father goes: Very nice.

And then, more silence. And then my father goes: You better call your mother.

And I'm like, I just got off the phone with her, she's the one who told me to call you.

And then my other line beeps. I go, hang on, it's Mommy. Actually, I'll call you back.

My mother: You should call your aunt, she had a fissure once. This is really terrible. I think she has a very good doctor.

I call my aunt. I tell her the whole story and she starts fucking howling. I'm like, Doda Sara, fuck you, this isn't funny. Mommy said you have a good doctor.

Doda Sara: I do have a good doctor. I have a very good doctor. And the office is right near where you live.

Me: What kind of a doctor does this kind of thing?

Doda Sara: A proctologist.

Me: Oh my god. I can't believe this. This is really a fucking nightmare. What sort of position does one have to get into to be examined for something like this?

She starts howling again, she's really cracking up when she says, the same position you were in when you got yourself into this situation to begin with.

I'm like, I really can't believe this. This has never happened to me before.

My aunt goes, don't worry, he's very good.

I go, what do you mean, *he*?

She goes, what do you mean, what do I mean?

Me: You go to a *male* proctologist?

Doda Sara: Yes.

Me: And don't tell me—he's Jewish too, right?

My aunt: Orthodox.

This is more than I can bear. *You go to an Orthodox male proctologist?*

And really, what could be better than me in a fucking waiting room surrounded by gray eighty-year-old Orthodox Jews?

As it turns out, Dr. Faigenblaum is in Israel for his grandson's bar mitzvah, so I have to see his associate, Dr. Horowitz. And as it turns out, what's better than me in a waiting room surrounded by gray eighty-year-old Orthodox Jews is me *buck naked* in Dr. Horowitz's office.

On top of everything else, like the fact that my ass is *killing me*, I am dying to poo. I can't decide whether

I should go now, before he gets in, or wait. There are pros and cons to both options. If I go now, at least I will have gone, but I don't have my baby wipes with me, so there might be some residue, which would obviously be perfectly revolting.

As I am contemplating this, Dr. Horowitz walks in.

He is *my age* and the biggest dork ever.

I am, at this point, really ready to die. Although he's not doing a very good job of it, Dr. Horowitz is trying to maintain a professional demeanor. It's not such a stretch to say that Dr. Horowitz looked *giddy* at the prospect of getting his filthy little hands into my ass. Remember that all his other patients are well into their eighties, while I, on the other hand, am offering a young, tight, pink butt hole for him to probe. And I could actually *see* his cock get hard when I told him that my problem, as it were, was a result of having had *anal sex.*

All this to say that sooner, rather than later, I was, as my aunt had promised, propped up *doggie style,* with Horowitz's gloved, lubed finger in my ass.

It's a bruised hemorrhoid, he says, with his finger still in my ass. Then he pulls his finger out of my ass and says to the nurse, scope, please. Out of the corner of my eye, I see the nurse hand over this thing that looks like a fucking three-foot-long telescope.

I'm like, *what* is that?

Horowitz goes, I'm just going to insert this to make sure.

I was like, *whoa*. I was like, *wait a second*. Is that really necessary?

And he goes, well, not really, I'm about ninety-five percent sure.

Not really?

I go, listen, ninety-five percent is good enough for me.

When I tell my mother that all I have is a bruised hemorrhoid and that Dr. Horowitz was a sexually aroused Orthodox Jew, she starts going, oh-my-god, oh my god. Peri, are you sure?

Me: Of course I'm sure.

My mother: How do you know?

Me: Because he had a hard-on, Mommy.

My mother: Oh-my-god. Oh my god.

And then she goes, wait. *Are you writing about this?*

Me: Obviously.

My mother: Oh my god. Oh my god, this is terrible. This is really terrible.

Me: Why is it terrible?

My mother: Oh my god. Peri, really, you can't do that. How can you do that? You can't write about this, it's very degrading.

Me: What are you talking about? It's totally normal.

I don't think that's very nice, my mother continued, what you're writing. You shouldn't say those kinds of things about your people. Non-Jews are going to read this and form opinions.

Me: So by telling the story about my hemorrhoid, I'm perpetuating anti-Semitism?

My mother: Yes.

part three

satanic verses, holy covenants

because I'm a New Yorker from New York, my perception of the city is different from, say, that of someone who moved here from Omaha. And though I live in Manhattan, I grew up in Queens, and once I was old enough to realize that I was in Queens and not in Manhattan, I knew that I was at a great disadvantage. I didn't want to live *near* the city. I wanted to live *in* the city. It is for this reason that I will never understand how people can get excited about, for example, moving to Brooklyn. Who gives a shit about Brooklyn? It's just another borough that *isn't* Manhattan. There's only one problem. Rent. The rent in Manhattan is fucking insane. But precisely because I'm not *from* Manhattan, I still have the same starry-eyed love for it that out-of-towners and tourists do.

As far as I'm concerned, if I'm going to live in New York, the only place to live is Manhattan. But if you want to live in Manhattan and you don't have twelve grand a month to blow on rent, your options become quite limited. You can move into a shoe box in a "cool" neighborhood (and still pay a fortune) or you can move into a slightly larger shoe box in a neighborhood that has not yet been gentrified, which is what I did. Not ideal, but not a bad deal either.

I live in a sixth-floor walk-up in East Harlem, four long blocks from the subway, with none of the amenities the rest of Manhattan offers. For example, nothing is within walking distance. No coffee shops, no stores, no decent supermarkets, in short, *nada*. You can't even hail a yellow cab. In a certain sense, East Harlem is like the last Shangri-la. In another sense, it is, essentially, the Queens of Manhattan.

Not too long ago, *The New York Times* ran some article called something like the "Upper Upper East Side," about my neighborhood. I thought it was very funny. The Upper East Side is one of the snottiest places in the world, with one of the most expensive zip codes in the country. There's no such thing as the "Upper Upper East Side." If the rest of Manhattan gives any indication, it might become so one day, but it certainly isn't yet. If you said "Upper Upper East Side" to people who consider East Harlem their stomping ground, they would laugh in your fucking face.

Which is to say that it's old school up here. While it's true that people are moving here from hipper neighborhoods and also true that white people started crawling out of the woodwork when the first bourgeois-y restaurant opened up, for the time being at least, East Harlem is *not* the Upper Upper East Side. For the time being, East Harlem still boasts its Latino flavor and the fact that it used to be (and still kind of is) a mob-dominated Italian-American neighborhood. If you doubt this for a minute, all you have to do is take note of the fact that you can buy homemade tamales on the street for a dollar or go to Patsy's, one of the oldest pizzerias in New York City and, quite possibly, the best pizzeria in New York City. There's the great Puerto Rican restaurant Sandy's and, of course, the legendary Italian restaurant Rao's. Because of Rao's, it is said, my block is the safest in New York City, and that very well may be true.

The week he moved to this neighborhood, a friend of mine walked by Rao's and popped in and was like, hey, I didn't know there was a restaurant here, I just moved in down the street, I'm going to have to come in and check it out sometime.

And the big, beefy guy inside goes, Buddy, we're all booked up.

And my friend, having never heard of Rao's, goes, you're all booked up? You're kidding.

And the big, beefy guy was like, no, I ain't kidding.

And my friend, still not getting it, was like, when are you booked until?

And the big, beefy guy goes, spring.

This was in early September.

Any weeknight that you walk past that place around dinnertime, you'll see limos and Town Cars and all the other cars that wiseguys drive. While they're inside Rao's, they leave their cars on the street. And when I say on the street, I mean just that—on the street. They're not parked, they're certainly not parked legally, and you can rest assured that nobody's getting a ticket.

I know all this because Rao's closes early, and the wiseguys who start off there make their way over to Barrone, which is where I used to waitress. The name is supposed to be pronounced "Bar One," because it's the first bar that opened in the neighborhood, but the Italians started calling it Barrone and, like most things the Italians do, it stuck.

There are about ten tables at Rao's, and they are owned—yes, owned—by the customers. If you want a table, you better know someone. If you don't know someone, you can forget about it. Or more to the point, you can fuggedaboud it.

I was once going to have dinner at Rao's with my ex-boyfriend Zevi, because he knows someone who has a table. What that means is that Zevi is from Brooklyn and, even though he is Israeli by birth, he is Italian, because all of his friends are Italian and he basically converted. I mean, if it's possible to convert from one ethnicity to another, Zevi has done it. Unfortunately, he wound up getting his driver's license revoked the day we were going to go, so we wound up not going. Which pissed both of us off, but what can you do? Not much. Not go to dinner at fucking Rao's, I'll tell you that much.

I lost my virginity to Zevi on the basement floor of his parents' house when I was seventeen. Recently, I was at my parents' house in Queens, cleaning out an old closet, and I found the bra and underwear I was wearing that first time we had sex. Cheap purple polyester panties accented with black lace. Matching bra. *Très chic.*

My mother, who was hovering over me while I was cleaning this closet, and monitoring my every move because she is a pack rat and god forbid I should throw anything away, was horrified when she saw this. She was like, this is the ugliest thing I have ever seen in my life, how could you wear that? What's wrong with you?

I was like, I lost my virginity in this thing. What do you mean, *what's wrong with me?* Nothing's wrong with me, give me a break. I was seventeen and I thought this was gorgeous, and anyway, Zevi loved it.

And even though we haven't had sex in, like, ten years, Zevi and I are still very close friends. When we were in high school, he looked like Marky Mark when Marky Mark was doing underwear ads. Which is to say, he was stocky and very muscular and not that tall and pretty fucking sexy. And in all fairness, he still is. Zevi apparently owns several businesses that he doesn't tell me about, but which I would not be at liberty to discuss even if he did.

This is the kind of thing he says to me: Hey, Pe', what da fuck is da matta wit you?

Zevi cannot, for the life of him, understand how I live my life.

A typical conversation between the two of us goes something like this:

Me: Hi, Zev, what are you doing?

Zevi: Eh, I gotta go to Tony's fuckin' engagement party, it's at his motha's house. Johnny got indicted by the feds and he's got one of them things around his ankle, so we gotta do it at Tony's motha's house because Johnny ain't allowed outta the house.

Me (fascinated): *Really?* What did Johnny do?

Zevi: Pe', don't ask me stoopid fuckin' questions on the phone. If you want to ask me dese questions when I see you, dat's another story.

Me: What's the difference? One thing in lieu of another.

Zevi: Hey, what are you? A fuckin' professor? Inloo. What da fuck is inloo? Listen to you, you think you're a big shot.

Me: Will you just fucking tell me what Johnny did.

Zevi: Pe', please, gimme a fuckin' break, will ya?

I was like, Zev, *please,* you have to tell me.

As it turns out, Johnny was involved in some sort of multimillion-dollar mail-fraud ring that was infiltrated by undercover cops, and while I probably shouldn't really be snouting around in things that are none of my business, I can't help it. By nature, I'm a very nosy person. Or not that I'm nosy, but I'm interested. I'm always very interested. I'm always very interested, and it is for this reason that I am constantly snouting around trying to listen to what people are saying. I suppose one could say I'm a lingerer, because I'm always lingering around trying to overhear things.

Working in a restaurant has proved a formidable way to do this. In part because people can't really give you a hard time. I mean, as a waitress, you're supposed to be hovering, and because you're supposed to be hovering, people have no idea that what you're *really* doing is gathering information.

Sometimes, however, hovering puts you in a position whereby *because* you have hovered, you have to engage in people's fucking idiocy. And believe me, a lot of people are morons. Either morons or alcoholics. If you learn nothing else from working in a restaurant, you learn that many,

many people have big drinking problems. Anyhow, had I not been hovering on this one night at Barrone, I probably would not have been summoned over to deal with this woman, who was drinking a glass of Pinot Grigio, and her guy, who was drinking a glass of the house Merlot.

Right off the bat, I could tell that these people were tedious. In general, it's fairly obvious who's tedious and who isn't, and these people were certainly tedious. Tedious, in this case, as in *sour*. She had mousy brown hair, and more generally, she looked like the kind of woman who hated sex. He looked like he couldn't believe his life had come to this. On top of that, you got the impression that they were not introspective at all. I thought there was a very good chance that in the years to come, one if not both of them would be putting personal ads up on craigslist.

In my mind, these people had very twisted and dark things going on. In real life, they had no sense of humor and were taking themselves *very* fucking seriously.

So this guy's looking at me, and then he's like, can I tell you something?

I was like, what? You're the cum pig, aren't you?

No, I didn't say that. What I did say was, sure. Because I'm the waitress, so what else can I say? I can't very well say, actually, whatever you're going to say is certainly going to bore me and I'm going to have to pretend to be interested, which is going to exhaust me, so why not just save us both the trouble? I obviously couldn't say that. So instead, I smile really big and am like, *sure*.

And he's like, um, you know, just a few pointers because you guys just opened up and you want things to go well. He was like, just a few pointers, about, um, the busboys.

He pauses. He's like, um, so you want to know?

I *hate* when people use "um" in this fashion. I hate when *I* use "um" in this fashion. Like as a filler. Like, I'm not going to say anything interesting and I'm actually a little nervous about saying what I am going to say and so I'm stalling—uuuhm. This is so fucking annoying. If you're going to say something, fucking say it and get behind it or shut the fuck up and don't say anything at all. The better way is to use it as a kind of linguistic foreplay. Like, I'm going to say something interesting, I'm working on it in my head, hold on a second, it'll be worth the wait.

To the cum pig I go, please, go ahead.

The cum pig looks at his girlfriend and is like, um, should I tell her?

And she's like, you already went this far, so you may as well.

And I'm like, please, by all means.

So he pauses again and goes, well, um, just a few little things. It's just, um, don't think I'm an asshole—

And I'm like, no, not at all, *of course not,* please go on.

And the guy goes, well, um, really, it was the pepper. The busboy asked me if I wanted pepper, but then, um, he didn't grind the pepper for me. Um, I had to grind the pepper myself.

I was like, I see.

He continues. Um, well, it's just that, um, the busboy should be the one who grinds the pepper. And he looks at his girlfriend and is like, I mean, they should know this, right?

And the woman was like, well, it's just, the busboy really could have been a little more confident with the pepper.

Um, also, the pseudo cum pig, who is definitely infinitely less interesting than the actual cum pig, continues, in most places the busboy will ask you if you're done with your water before he takes it away, and even though there was only a little bit left in my glass, um, he just took it.

And at first, before he pled his case, I'm looking at this guy, wondering if there was any chance this was going to be something worth telling the busboys. And the cum pig, I suppose he was nice enough, I mean, he wasn't *trying* to be a dick or anything, but then, after he pled his case, instead of thanking him for wasting my time and telling him he should really consider getting a fucking life, I made a joke and was like, should I be concerned about what you're going to say to the busboys about me?

Ha ha, I laughed. I'm not good at faking laughter.

Ha ha, he laughed, he was like, um, I hope you don't think I'm an asshole.

And I was like, *nooooo*, not at all, of course not.

And then I said, don't worry, I'll *definitely* talk to the busboys and take care of this, and in the meantime, perhaps you would like me to shove the pepper mill up your ass? Like I fucking give a shit about your fucking pepper. Like I'm in a restaurant full of mobsters who are slipping me hundred-dollar bills for bringing them a *fucking napkin*, do you honestly think I don't have more interesting things to think about than the fact that you had to grind your own fucking pepper?

I mean, really. The shit I have to put up with. But things balance out, because on other days I have the pleasure of dealing with people like "Big Six."

Big Six was originally known as "Six Fingers" or just "Six," because he always had a cigarette in his hand, but when he quit smoking he gained like four hundred pounds and everyone started calling him Big Six. Then he started smoking again and lost some of the weight, but "Big Six" kind of stuck even though most people just called him Six.

Six stands about five-foot-five and is, shall we say, stout. In the dead of winter, Six is tan. He is tan in the way only someone who spends a good deal of time in a tanning salon is tan. As in *orange*.

He has the same coloring as the girl with whom boyfriend from college cheated on me when I went to London for three weeks. When I got back, my boyfriend and I had sex, and then he went into the bathroom to take a shower and I rolled over onto an empty condom wrapper. I shouted toward the bathroom, babe, what's this? And he came out from the shower and looked at it and said, that's from us.

I was like, but we don't use condoms.

But this isn't about my heartbreak. This is about Big Six, who may not be big insofar as his height is concerned but is a big wiseguy nevertheless, and who, along with his orange skin, has bleached blond hair and enormous white-capped teeth.

It was after eleven in the morning and the place was packed because it was what they call "Marathon Sunday." So after a Saturday night of moderate to fairly heavy drinking, I had gotten up at nine o'clock in order to serve people like Six and his friends brunch while they watched thousands of people run twenty-six-plus miles. Barrone is located in such a place that the runners actually run right by the joint.

Which is to say that thousands of people were literally running right past us. And we were watching it live on TV as well. And Six was there with his pockmarked, deferential friend Sonny, and after they had finished eating brunch, he and Six, who on this day was wearing a bright yellow fleece, went outside. I went out too and I was standing next to him and we were watching all these fucking people run through Spanish Harlem toward the Bronx.

I was like, oh my god, there are so many people, I've

never seen anything like this, they look like those suicidal animals that run off the mountains in packs. I mean, there must be thousands of them.

And Six starts roaring and goes, yeah! Shit, yeah! Tou-sandz. Tenz a tou-sandz. Fuck dat, hundredz a tousandz.

And then Six goes, hey, Sonny, willya take a look at dat cop?

"Dat cop" was this elderly policeman standing halfway across the street from us. And the cop was kind of short and chubby.

Six is going, next time I rob someone, I want dat fuckin' guy to chase me.

At this, Sonny began to howl. But then Sonny howls whenever Six says *anything*, so it's hard to tell whether Sonny howls because he really thinks Six is funny or because Six is his boss and that's what he's supposed to do.

Six was like, ain't dere a height requirement to be a cop? Dis guy looks like someone dropped a safe on his head!

The way Sonny was laughing, you would think this was the funniest thing he had heard in his entire life.

Six lit a cigarette and was blowing smoke in the runners' direction, and then he got all animated and started waving his arms around and he turns to me and goes, hey, Dollface, wouldya get me anodder Bloody Mary?

According to Six and his compatriots, I'm Dollface. Dollface.

Fitting, don't you think? Initially, this irritated me. I mean, I don't really take that kindly to being called things like "Dollface." But because it was Six, I figured it would behoove me to keep my mouth shut.

So I'm Dollface, and I'm also "Sey-rah!" because all the wiseguys think I look like the actress Sarah Jessica Parker, which is totally fucking irritating. It's irritating because it's not true, and it's annoying, because even though I like Sarah Jessica Parker's outfits, I don't like hearing that I look like her every fucking day.

Anyway, there were people running past us this whole time, and when we saw on TV that someone had finished, in two hours and eight minutes, Six starts shouting, two fuckin' hours! I can't even drive that fast! Willya look at dat guy? Willya look at him? Dat guy's gotta be from Kenya or sumtin'.

I found this whole thing to be quite unbelievable. Unbelievable because on the one hand this seemed like a very racist thing to say, though it wasn't, necessarily. I mean, it's not like the Dutch are the ones constantly winning marathons.

But then this Puerto Rican chick walked by and Six was like, 'ey! Dollface!

And I was like, *hey!* I thought *I* was Dollface.

But I didn't say that either.

Later that day, Six came up to me while I was on break, and was like, Sey-rah! Sey-rah! Can I ask you sumtin' serious?

So I go, of course.

Which opened the fucking floodgates. Six starts going on and on about losing weight and quitting cigarettes and eating a better diet, and then he stops and he goes, Periel, seriously. Willya do me a fayvah? Willya make me a list? You know, of food I can eat to lose weight.

And I was like, sure, Six, sure, no problem.

And he goes, next time I come in, you give it to me, okay?

And then he lowers his voice and goes, but don't let none of my friends see you do it, okay? Cuz dey'll make fun of me.

I almost died when he said that.

Here you have this fucking tough guy asking me to

make him a list—he goes, Monday through Friday, no, actually, make it seven days, I always think Monday through Friday, but on second thought, it should be seven days—but he doesn't want any of his friends to know because they'll make fun of him.

You can chain-smoke and cheat on your wife and do coke and tear up hundred-dollar bills and fuck hookers and burn cars and kill people and nobody says a word, but you go on a diet, and, for that, they'll give you a hard time.

I informed Six that it would be my pleasure to make him such a list, and even though he always seemed to kind of adore me, I got a sense that saying yes to that *really* put me in his good graces. Which, all things considered, is a good place to be. It came in handy especially when this wiseguy I had never seen before walked in, looked me up and down, and said, getchya coat, we're leavin'.

I was like, ha ha, that's very funny.

And the wiseguy goes, I ain't kidding. Getchya coat, we're leavin'.

I looked at Six, who growled at him and said, 'ey, Jimmy, leav'er da fuck alone, and that was the end of that.

One day when my shift ended, I sat down at the bar to have a drink and wait for Kat, who was supposed to come meet me, when Chip, the half-pint bartender who can barely see over the bar, starts harassing me with his fucking bullshit. Chip is the kind of person who comes in on his day off, sits at the bar all night sucking down gin and tonics with no ice, and then, one minute before the kitchen is about to close, orders a pork chop.

Chip tends bar in the restaurant, which means that he knows the kitchen closes at midnight. So if you know that the kitchen closes at midnight, then you also know that the kitchen is not some arbitrary otherworldly thing. And if you know that the kitchen is not some arbitrary otherworldly thing, then you know too that there are actually *people* who work back there and you know that the *people* who work in the kitchen have been there for like twenty hours, which means that they don't need you coming along, night after fucking night, at eleven fifty-nine and ordering a fucking pork chop.

If you learn anything from working in a restaurant, it's that the guys who work in the kitchen work like fucking dogs and are, like, *dead* by the end of the night.

If you know anything at all, and if you have even just one grain of fucking integrity, you know that the last thing these people want to be doing is grilling up a fucking pork chop at midnight.

On top of all this, Chip is under the delusional impression that he's some kind of Oscar-winning director, so he's always trying to act like one, which is actually one of the most tedious things I have ever encountered.

Every time I look at him, I can't help picturing him going home and shutting his bedroom door, putting on a beret and an ascot, hopping up onto a step stool, sitting down and crossing his legs, and gazing at himself in the mirror, imagining that he's in a director's chair.

So we're both at the bar and I'm waiting for Kat when Chip starts in with: Periel, I need to ask you a very strange question.

Me: Yes, Chip?

And Chip goes, you know how I'm casting a movie, right?

This is *exactly* what I'm talking about with this fucking guy. How would I know that he was "casting a movie," and even if I did, why would he assume that I did? I mean, he never told me this, so what—did he figure word just got around? There's a real fucking buzz,

Chip is "directing" a movie. Who the fuck do you think you are, Francis fucking Ford Coppola?

So I go, no, Chip, I didn't.

And he's like, well, you *do* know that I'm a director, right? He's like, I'm a director [he really *is* this pretentious] and I'm casting this movie and we're shooting this scene on Thursday—

I'm like, wait. You're shooting but you haven't finished casting yet?

And he was like—actually, I have no recollection of how he responded to that, but he went on to say that he wanted me to make some shirts, like the ones I had made for myself and worn to work, for two of the dumb actresses in this so-called movie of his, which is called something like *The Lost Shoe*—about a boy who gets lost in a cave and loses his fucking shoe.

And then—and this was the best part—he goes, and I'd give you credit. Like in the credits, it would say that you did the costumes or whatever. He was like, I don't know if that's what you want to do, be a costume designer or whatever, but it would be a good opportunity.

He's telling me this as though *my* doing *him* this favor would be *his* doing *me* a favor. He was like, one of the girls is a size four and the other is a six.

This *enraged* me. But I tried to respond nicely. I mean, I was trying to be very civilized. It's not that I blame him for wanting me to do this, I can whip up some real gems on the sewing machine thanks to Mari, but making clothes for people no one has ever fucking heard of, for a movie that no one will ever see, that will be or is in the process of being directed by fucking Chip, is not exactly my idea of publicity. And it wasn't the request so much that bothered me—I mean, the request in and of itself was fine—but for the love of god, talk about delusions of fucking grandeur.

So he goes, well, why don't you come down to fit the girls? You could come to the shoot in Williamsburg at nine o'clock Thursday morning.

I was like, let me think about that. No.

I was like, I don't think so. I was like, I don't fucking think so at all.

Here I am, trying so hard not to be an asshole and this guy has the nerve, the fucking audacity, to tell me I should come to him? At nine in the morning, no less. I was like, I don't go anywhere at nine in the morning. And I'm *certainly* not schlepping out to fucking Williamsburg, Brooklyn, which is a hipster nightmare at any time of day.

And he was like, well, what about tomorrow, then?

So I was like, no, tomorrow's no good.

And he was like, well, you could give me something now and I could see if it fits them and then I could give it back to you.

And I was like, Chip, I'm in a bar, you know? I don't have a dress in my fucking pocket.

And then, and this is just the best, he got all whiny and shit and was like, well, you do live right up the street.

As though I'm going to fucking run home and up five flights of stairs for this guy.

So I was like, look. I was like, if you want me to make you something, I will. If you want me to make you clothes for your movie, I already said I would, but these things don't appear from the sky. I mean, it takes a little while. For example, we would need material.

And he goes, oh, no problem, just get the fabric and keep the receipt and I'll write it off from the expense account.

Oh, yeah, sure, no problem, why don't I just dash off into the heart of the garment district and have everything for you by, let's say, nine a.m. tomorrow? How's that, Chip? I'll have everything on your desk, even though you probably don't even have a desk, first thing tomorrow morning.

Can you fucking imagine? I mean, the nerve of some people is, like, really astounding. And obviously there is some insecurity here. Obviously, Chip is a person who is insecure with his level of success (or lack thereof) and is trying to overcompensate. Which is fine, even though it's actually *not* fine, because what it really is, is pretty fucking pathetic. I can't stand these kinds of egomaniacs who pretend that they're not egomaniacs. Especially because it's so fucking transparent. I mean, you can always tell who's an egomaniac and who isn't.

For example, me. I'm definitely an egomaniac, but at least I don't walk around pretending that I'm *not* an egomaniac. At least I know that being an egomaniac is a ridiculous thing to be. Chip's an egomaniac without even a shred of irony. And I'll tell you something else, so is Salman Rushdie.

Or anyway, this was the impression I got when I saw him walking in SoHo a while ago flanked by his young, hot girlfriend.

Salman Rushdie was strutting down Prince Street, wearing a dark, longish coat that I have to assume was cashmere. He was balding, and wearing sunglasses when there was no reason to be wearing sunglasses. He was large in front, which means his belly protruded, and this hot young girlfriend was bopping alongside him. I surmised that the hot young girlfriend was Salman Rushdie's girlfriend because in the nail salon I had recently read an article about how Salman Rushdie had a hot young girlfriend. The girlfriend looked very pleased to be bopping alongside Salman Rushdie. She also looked like she was thinking about all the expensive things Salman Rushdie was about to buy her.

Salman Rushdie, on the other hand, did not look like he was thinking about all the expensive things he was about to buy his hot young girlfriend. He looked like he was thinking, *I am Salman Rushdie.*

He looked like he was thinking, *I am Salman Rushdie and I cannot believe that I am Salman Rushdie.* He looked like he was thinking, *I am Salman Rushdie and I can hardly believe what good fortune I have to be Salman Rushdie.*

Salman Rushdie, flanked by his hot young girlfriend, looked like he was thinking all of these things. Salman Rushdie, flanked by his hot young girlfriend, did not look the slightest bit concerned about the fact that he had a *fatwa* on his head, which made me think that perhaps he no longer did. I later did some investigating and found that the *fatwa* still exists but only, really, as a gesture. No one is going to actually carry it out.

Salman Rushdie looked sort of in awe of himself. You want to know how he looked? He looked smug, that's how he fucking looked. He looked like he had no idea that someone as nosy as me was watching him in very stalkerlike fashion.

Which I took as a very bad sign. If I'm watching you and you don't know that I'm watching you, you're fucking zoned out. And that's bad. Because if you're zoned out, then you're not on top of your game, and if you're not on top of your game, then you're vulnerable. And it's when you're vulnerable that the sexual sadists, the sociopaths, and the necrophiliacs swoop in to hack you up, so they can arrange the pieces of your dead body into some crazy pose or fuck your corpse.

You think I'm crazy, you think I'm exaggerating? I am very sensitive to things like this. I'm not crazy and I'm not exaggerating. And if you think I am, it just shows how ignorant you are. Pick up any John Douglas book and you'll quickly realize that sexual homicides are on the rise and that you should be extremely cautious, because people are out of their fucking minds. Anyone who knows anything knows that a streak of violence lurks right beneath the surface and that the very people you think are the nicest would actually love nothing more than to torture you to death.

Kat tells me, Periel, you're *so* paranoid.

I'm like, no shit. *Of course* I'm paranoid. You should be too.

I somehow missed the boat for typical Jewish neuroses and jumped straight into hard-core paranoia. For the most part I have my paranoia in check, but in certain situations it seriously cramps my style.

Like every time I get on a plane. Whenever I leave the state, my parents insist on seeing me off at the airport. Sometimes this is very comforting, and other times it's very problematic. It's comforting because if I die, at least I'll have had my last moments with them, but it's problematic because between their neuroses and my paranoia, things can really get out of hand.

Like the time I was on line at the check-in counter at La Guardia with my parents in tow when I spotted this tall, shady-looking Arab-looking dude, in a bright baby-blue kind of gangsta jogging suit, with a beard, two plastic bags, no luggage, and a black ski hat, about five people in front of me. I turned to my mother and was like, Mommy, that guy looks totally shady.

And she was like, what? who?

And I was like, who? I was like, who? The tall shady-looking fucking Arab who looks like a terrorist, that's fucking who. Who the fuck do you think?

And she turns to my father and goes, Michael. Michael, look.

And my father goes, you're being prejudiced.

And I was like, that very well may be the case, but I can tell you right now that I am more certain than I have ever been of anything in my entire life that if that guy gets on my plane, there's not a chance in hell I'm getting on it.

Then the shady Arab with no luggage goes up to the ticket counter and pulls out a wad of cash the size of Sri Lanka.

So my mom goes, I'm going to see what's going on here, and she actually goes up to the ticket counter and says, excuse me, but who is that man?

And of course the guy at the ticket counter is half brain-dead and is like, what man?

And my mom is like, the man in the blue outfit, where is he going?

And the half-brain-dead guy at the ticket counter is like, that information is confidential, ma'am.

And my mother, of course, is totally fucking shameless about this. She goes—and she actually said this—well, I'd like to know, because he looks like an unsavory character.

And the half-brain-dead ticket counter guy is like, don't worry, ma'am, I know him, and anyway he's going to be screened.

So my mom comes back and tells us this as though it actually means something.

And then my dad's like, not everyone in this line is going to the same place, pumpkin.

And I'm like a raving lunatic right now. I'm like, I don't give a fuck, I'm telling you right now that I'm not getting on that plane. I was like, you have to be a total moron to get on a plane with that guy, you have to have a death wish, you have to be, like, the biggest moron in the entire world to get on a plane with that guy.

So then my dad spots these undercover cops, and, of course he's thrilled at the prospect of talking to them, and who the hell would have known they're undercover cops except for my father? So he makes his way over to them and apparently voices his, or rather my, concern that there is a potential terrorist or at the very least someone who looks like one wandering around the airport, and they're like, yeah, well, don't worry, because we'll check it out. They're like, you know, we're not supposed to do racial profiling, but whatever.

So my dad comes back and reports this as though *this* actually means something, and I'm like, Pa, that doesn't fucking translate into anything. What does that mean? That doesn't fucking mean anything.

And my mother is going, LANGUAGE, Peri! Please! Do you have to use such language?

At this point, I am on the brink of losing it and I'm like, you know what? I'm taking matters into my own fucking hands. I decide the only thing to do is to stake out the gate and stare down every motherfucker who gets on that plane, and if the terrorist boards, I'm out and that's the fucking end of it.

So I say good-bye to my parents and head through security. The security bitch with the wand stops me and makes me open my Prada bag so she can further investigate what was apparently a suspicious-looking item. I don't mind this at all——I like the illusion of safety——but I'm like, could you please be a little bit more careful with my bag, please? I paid a good deal of money so I can walk around with this little triangle that says "Prada." I was like, please be a bit more careful, as I paid more for this bag than what most Haitians make in a year, and I need it lest I forget that I live in a social trance and am a complete fashion victim.

And the security bitch was like, take your boots off.

So I did.

Then I gathered my boots and my bag and proceeded to my gate, and like a fucking hawk, I scoped out the entire scene. I wasn't the only one on terrorist watch, which reassured me that I was not paranoid, but rather, a person with an acute sense of awareness. I mean, obviously I'm on to something if I'm looking for terrorists along with three military guys, each armed with a machine gun the size of my leg. Other than their enviable camouflage outfits and the fact that they were packing heat, these guys had nothing on me. I mean, they were doing the same fucking thing I was doing. Looking. Big fucking deal.

So I'm sitting there, bugging out, when it occurs to me that obviously my terrorist is not going to be gallivanting around the waiting area. Obviously he is going to be piddling around somewhere else until the very last moment so as to cover his tracks. I decide to go smoke a cigarette.

When I get back to the gate, I resume my position. People are now starting to board, and my terrorist guy is still nowhere to be seen. I figure it's now or never, so I get up to get on line, when this other Arab-looking dude, this clean-shaven Arab dude, also with no hand luggage, gets on line behind me.

I start to freak out all over again—who the fuck travels without hand luggage? As far as I can tell, the only explanation for getting on a plane with no hand luggage is that you're going to blow the plane up. So I *leave* the line to check him out from a distance, and I see that he's holding a book, a hardcover book with gold script all over it, and become absolutely convinced that this book is the Koran. It's abundantly clear to me that if this book is, in fact, the Koran, then there is really not a chance in hell I'm going to get on this plane.

So, like an animal circling its prey, I start circling him. I'm trying to make out what the book is, but the guy's hand is covering the title. For some reason, I am suddenly very calm. Or not for *some* reason, but for the specific reason that the three Valium I recently ingested have finally kicked in. Now I am brave.

So I get back on line and I'm right behind the Koran guy, and the whole time I'm still craning my neck to see if it's the Koran, in which case I figure I can just book it back to the gate. As I'm craning my neck to make out the title of the book, I see that his passport is not from Saudi Arabia or Egypt or any other terrorist-den country, but rather the Republic of India.

This makes me feel schmaltzy. I love India. I grew up in a neighborhood filled with Indians, and when I finally went to India, I really fell in love with the country. Among other things, going to India makes you understand, if you didn't before, why having a Prada bag is the most odious thing in the world. So I feel like an asshole and I smile at the Arab guy with the book, who is, in final analysis, not Arab at all. He smiles back, and I see that the book he was holding, the book I thought was the Koran, is *not* the Koran, but Salman Rushdie's *The Satanic Verses*. I couldn't believe it. But because I had racially profiled him and so erroneously cast judgment, I forgave him for reading this book, and figured I should probably read it myself since I've talked so much shit about its author.

So it turned out that that guy wasn't shady. But my other guy, with the beard and the hat and the baby-blue gangsta jogging outfit and the plastic bags and the wad of cash the size of Sri Lanka, who disappeared into the nowhere of the airport, I remain convinced, was shady. Or maybe not.

I suppose it's entirely possible that he was some sort of British hip-hop mogul who was carrying a sandwich. Which is both the point and the problem with being paranoid—innocent people fall victim to your paranoia. This is exactly what happened to poor Ali, a former co-waiter of mine. Ali was a very nice guy and a terrible waiter. Once, when he was trying to uncork a bottle of wine and couldn't get it open, he stood in front of his table of customers and actually put the bottle between his legs, and then, with his irritating English accent, said, it's a bit stuck. . . .

Poor Ali left England and flew to the United States to try to become an actor. Poor Ali, who is of Pakistani descent, though much, *much* more Arab-looking than scatological Nadir, who doesn't look Arab at all, even though there would be no reason for either one to look like an Arab, since Pakistanis aren't even Arabs to begin with, which is something I found out only when I called

Nadir a dirty Arab and he said, "Mama might be dirty, but she's not an Arab."

In any event, Nadir looks neither Pakistani nor Arab nor like a terrorist, unlike Ali, who looks very much like an Arab and also very much like a terrorist, in spite of the fact that he is neither.

Poor Ali, with his dark complexion and big nose and his unruly facial hair, looks a good deal like that shoe bomber, Richard Reid, and therefore really *does* look like a terrorist. And unfortunately for him, I'm not the only one who thinks so, which is why, when he flew from London to New York to audition at the Actors Studio, unbeknownst to him, three fighter jets were hovering above his plane as it crossed the Atlantic. When the plane landed, three FBI agents boarded the plane and approached him while he was still in his seat, and were like, Ali Mussai?

And Ali, whose last name *is* Mussai, was like, yes?

And they were like, will you please come with us?

Will you please come with us? was something that they *asked* but obviously didn't really *mean*. It wasn't like they were really asking him, it wasn't like he could have said, no, actually, fuck off, I won't come with you. And thus, they escorted him off the plane, to where several other people greeted him. More FBI, and a couple of NYPD. Except that he wasn't really greeted—more like cuffed—and then one of the guys dug two fingers under Ali's armpit and escorted him into an interrogation room, where they kept him for four and a half hours, asking him questions like, what do you think of September eleventh?

What had happened was that they thought Ali was one of the top ten Al Qaeda suspects, which, to judge solely from his looks, was entirely possible. But as we all know, outside of being totally fucking racist, judging someone solely on looks is a bit shallow. In any event, they pulled poor Ali into this interrogation room and they were like, blah, blah, blah, are you a member of Al Qaeda?

He was like, no, I am not a member of Al Qaeda.

And then they were like, hmm. They were like, hmm, that's odd, because you certainly *look* like you're a member of Al Qaeda.

They didn't really say that, but you can bet your ass it's what they were thinking. What they did say was: What do your parents do? And then, are they religious? And, where do they live?

And Ali was like, my parents are lawyers, and no, they are not religious, and they live in London.

And they were like, do you have any family here?

Yes, I do.

Who?

And Ali was like, my sister.

And they were like, is *she* religious?

Yes.

How religious?

And he was like, well, quite religious.

How religious?

And he was like, extremely religious.

And they were like, what does that mean?

And he was like, she prays five times a day and wears one of those fucking things on her head.

At which point they were like, well, buddy, you're pretty much *fucked*.

Ali's Muslim sister lives in Queens with her religious Muslim husband and their three kids, and is by all accounts a religious fundamentalist. Which doesn't necessarily mean that she and her religious fundamentalist husband *are* terrorists, but the fact is that Ali's plane got escorted from Heathrow to JFK by fighter jets because the FBI thought he was a terrorist because he looks like one, which very well may be the most fucked-up thing ever but is true nevertheless.

Ali eventually left the restaurant to pursue acting full-time, which was a wise move on his part because (a) he was a terrible waiter, and (b) there is, I am sure, going to be a high demand for actors who look like terrorists when they make a Hollywood movie about September 11 and the war in Iraq.

As far as his sister is concerned, I imagine she is still in Queens, wrapped up in a burka and praying five times a day.

I think the first time Kat told me I was paranoid was when we were driving back from wherever the fuck we were going when she got that ticket for speeding like a fucking lunatic in Vermont. She pulled over for gas, and was like, will you go inside and pay?

And I was like, yeah, sure. And I started taking my earrings out, the big silver hoops with my name in Hebrew that Brooke Fenster-Bloom was so fond of.

Kat was like, Periel, what are you doing?

I was like, I'm taking my earrings out.

Kat goes, I know you're taking your earrings out, why on earth?

Did you see the guy behind the counter? He looks like Osama bin Laden's little brother. Which he did. And nothing against Osama bin Laden's little brother, I imagine there are some members of the bin Laden family who don't hate Jews, but sometimes it's good not to tempt fate. Or not tempt fate. I don't even know what tempting fate means. Whatever. But if this country is in the middle of murdering Iraqis, and I'm walking into a fucking store with a bearded, turbaned fucking Arab behind the counter, it doesn't seem all that wise to walk in wearing enormous earrings with Hebrew lettering. I was like, Jesus, Kat, use some common sense.

So my phone rang and this charming woman started telling me she had seen my shirts and she wanted me to design shirts for her AIDS campaign. She said, hello, darling, I saw your shirts and I nearly dropped dead on the spot. The deal was that this woman, Leigh Blake, founded this organization, called Keep A Child Alive, which enlists the public to buy anti-retroviral drugs that go directly to clinics in Africa. And the shirts she wanted me to design would say "Drug Dealer" on them, which I thought was a brilliant fucking idea.

Because who the fuck else can we count on? Certainly not the governments. *Certainly* not the fucking pharmaceutical companies. This direct exchange between the public and the clinics works brilliantly. All I do is make the shirts, sell them, and keep the money for Prada bags. I'm kidding. All the money from the shirts goes to Keep A Child Alive. Obviously.

When the first shirts were ready, there was a photo shoot. And everyone came out in droves: makeup artists, photographers, hairstylists, models, celebrities, etc. Things were running very smoothly until one large-breasted famous actress breezes in, with an entourage of like forty people. Her assistant looks at the "Drug Dealer" tank top and informs me that she cannot put it on because—ready?—*because it will ruin her hair.*

I look at said famous actress and go, you can stretch the neck out, I think it'll be okay.

Said famous actress looks at me but does not say

anything. And although she is looking at me, I can't tell if she really sees me. Said famous actress has had so much plastic surgery that she does not really look like a person but like a thing. Like a blow-up doll, really. While said famous actress is silent, her homosexual assistant offers, look, she can't put the shirt on, she has a party to go to after this and she can't mess up her hair.

I'm like, oh, I get it. Millions of people are dying of AIDS, and as a homosexual male who would have likely been dead if you had been around in the eighties, because you're obviously a fucking slut, you're more concerned about her hair getting messed up than in her posing in this fucking shirt, which is what she's fucking here for? Got it.

So we end up lopping off the top of an XL men's T-shirt so nothing would touch her hair, which isn't even her real hair to begin with, and then, as a finishing touch, we tie a bow around her waist. When we emerge from the dressing room, her entourage breaks out in applause and someone on her payroll squeals, you look precious—you look like a little gift!

I refrain from pointing out, just as I did when Kat gave me the coffee drink, that a gift is an act of aggression.

Shortly after a tsunami claims close to 300,000 lives in the Indian Ocean, I am required to go to my cousin's birthday party. It's not so much that I'm required, but as my father puts it, going is "the right thing to do." I'm not so concerned about the fact that it's the right thing to do, but I figure I may as well stop by and offer my best wishes. This is already in the aftermath of a big to-do with my mother, who told me she was going to buy my cousin a key chain from Tiffany's.

I was like, I'm so fucking sure you're going to get him a key chain from Tiffany's. The guy's a fucking corporate lawyer, I'm so sure he needs a fucking key chain from Tiffany's. I was like, let me tell you something. You are *not* going to get him a key chain from Tiffany's. What you are going to do is make a fucking donation to one of these tsunami relief funds in his name. Or not in his name, but you'll write on the card that that's what you did.

My mother is going, LANGUAGE, Peri, please! LANGUAGE. I'll talk to your father.

I'm like, there's nothing to talk about. Do it.

This is the same cousin who, mind you, I had a fucking brawl with after my grandfather's funeral because he was saying that we were right in going into Iraq. I'm talking, like, serious brawl. This is the same cousin who is not only a corporate lawyer but also a Republican who is very into Judaism. He's a Republican, he's all Zionistic, and his girlfriend is not Jewish. I asked my mother one time, who gives a shit if he keeps kosher at dinner, when he's eating Gentile pussy for dessert? My mother had an absolute fit when I said this—oh my god, oh my god, what a terrible thing to say, how awful—and on and on it went until I was finally like, look, it is not a terrible thing to say. It's not terrible at all, and for her sake, I *hope* he's eating Gentile pussy for dessert.

Because of the political divide, my relationship with him is a bit strained. I happen to be extremely fond of his girlfriend, who is not a Republican, and in spite of myself, I like him too, so I try to make it so that he and I can get along. It's difficult, but usually he keeps his political views to himself, so I try to keep my mouth shut on those matters as well.

Except at his birthday party, I was telling my father how Susan Sarandon had left me a ticket for the next night to go see her discuss her work as an activist and my cousin, whom no one was even talking to, goes, I'd like to tell Susan Sarandon to go fuck herself.

I smiled and very sweetly said, if it wasn't your birthday, I would tell *you* to go fuck *yourself,* but in the meantime, I'll be sure to pass that message along to Ms. Sarandon, who I'm certain will be absolutely fascinated.

This is the same night I overheard his friends saying, I know that there are hundreds of thousands of people that were affected by the tsunami, and it's awful, but Jerry Orbach's death just affected me much more on a personal level. *Law & Order* is maybe my favorite show, and I feel like I lost a friend, you know?

No. I do not know. Who the fuck is Jerry Orbach?

In the car on the way home, I report this to my mother, who replies, what can I tell you, it's a very sad commentary on our culture.

After a few minutes, she goes: There has to be some kind of improvement here, because it's getting worse and worse and it's very sad.

I'm like, what, Jerry Orbach's death or the tsunami?

And my mother goes, no, I'm talking about your hair.

And I go, *you're talking about my hair?*

And my mother goes, when someone is blessed with something like good genes or talent and abuses it or wastes it, it's really a crime, and that's what you do with your hair when you don't brush it, which you never do.

It's terrible. I bought you a comb, and you better start using it, because I can't take this anymore.

I go, Mommy, I really cannot fathom why we are having this conversation.

My mother goes, you behave like a preadolescent. I tried so hard to bring you up properly, and this is how you behave, it's terrible. It's really terrible. I'm buying you a detangler, and you are going to use it because I can't stand this anymore, you look dirty.

I go, I don't even know what a detangler is.

My mother goes, I know! That's the whole problem! You don't know and you don't want to know. You don't want to do anything except smoke cigarettes, go shopping, talk about serial killers and disgusting things that happen on the Internet. You're obsessed with lowlifes and filth. And you use foul language. I'm very concerned about you. And you're too skinny. I'm sure you're not eating properly.

I'm like, Mommy, this is actually really outrageous, there is something wrong with you. I'm telling you about the tsunami, and you're talking to me about all of this bullshit and my hair?

My mother goes, I'm telling you about your hair because when you walked into the party, I noticed immediately that it looked very disheveled. People would *die* for hair like yours, and it's not right. If you don't do something drastic, you're going to have dull, disgusting, scraggly-looking hair. When I think of all the money I spent on you, going to waste.

I'm like, all of it?

My mother: Most of it. Not all of it.

Me: Because of my hair.

My mother: And because you smoke pot.

Me: I haven't smoked pot in like five years. And for the record, I happen to think I turned out pretty well. Given what's happened to most of the people I grew up with, I happen to think I turned out pretty fucking okay. I mean, Queens isn't exactly a breeding ground for success. Think of Fizzle.

My mother goes, who?

I go, Fizzle, you remember Fizzle, don't you?

My mother did not remember Fizzle, so I was like, you know what, never mind.

I knew Zevi would remember Fizzle, because when Zevi and I used to date, we would hang out with him all the time. So after I got home from the party, I called Zevi, because I thought he would want to know that Fizzle was in trouble.

I say, I think Fizzle is going to jail.

Zevi goes, listen, Pe', I got enough people in jail, I don't need to hear about this shit.

I go, well, don't you even want to know what happened?

Zevi: I gotta be honest, I don't really give a shit.

I'm like, Zev, come on, this is terrible, he was set up—some money-laundering thing.

Zevi goes, oh, no big deal, white-collar.

Zevi had recently gotten engaged. He had gotten engaged, which means he was doing what he was "supposed" to be doing, and it is for this reason that he feels, more than ever, that I have really got to pull it together.

Zevi's going, there's something really fuckin' wrong wit' you, Pe'. Your world ain't normal.

Me: My world is fucking normal.

Your world is normal for fucking lesbians and faggots, he says. What the fuck is da matta wit' you, Pe'? You gotta settle down.

I go, what the fuck do you want from me? You want me to get pregnant and become a childbearing vessel to perpetuate a totally fucking corrupt economic system?

Zevi: Oh boy, here we go. Listen. Don't fucking bullshit me with all this crap dat's in your head. You don't got eighty years to think about this shit, you're gonna be dead.

So you want me to put on a white dress?

I don't give a shit what color dress you put on— knowing you, you'd probably wear black, you Satanist bitch.

I really lost it when he said that—I started laughing so hard I could barely talk. I was like, you are so funny, I can't stand it.

He goes, what's funny, Pe'? You're laughing at yourself. I'm just stating what you're doing wit' ya life.

I'm like, wait, wait, Zev, seriously, I need to get a pen.

And he goes, I can't talk to you no more, every time I say something, you gotta write it down.

I go, now you sound like my mother.

One Saturday night, I call Kat to tell her I'm walking past the church of Latter-day Saints, and she says,

I haven't been there in months, but I'll be there to-morrow.

When I ask her what she's doing tonight, she tells me she's on her way to her sister's house, where there is a bottle of Russian cognac waiting.

I'm like, you're going to slug back a bottle of cognac and then you're going to church tomorrow?

Kat goes, well, I've decided that I don't really see why the two have to be mutually exclusive.

Isn't that what I've been trying to tell you?

She's like, I guess. I mean, sometimes I feel guilty when I'm smoking a cigarette and carrying my yoga mat, but then I think, what? So I should stop doing yoga because I smoke? Clearly not.

I go, that's what I've been trying to tell you for two years.

as it turns out, the night after the bottle of cognac, Kat did not find her way to the Lord's house. Rather, she found her way to our favorite discount store, Century 21, where I scored a pair of dramatically reduced Dolce & Gabbana boots. What can I say? For all my activism, I have a total shopping disorder and like Walt Whitman said of himself, I am large, I contain multitudes, and I wallow in my inconsistency. Or like Roland Barthes said in *The Fashion System*, those who exclude themselves from fashion, which is a social fact, "suffer a sanction: the stigma of being unfashionable." And who the fuck wants to be that?

At least I'm fucking aware of my weakness for haute couture, and I know it can really get out of hand. Like the time Kat convinced me to go with her to a wedding in Secaucus, which is like in the crotch of the New Jersey Turnpike, by promising she would drive me first to the Secaucus outpost of Century 21. This was a big deal, since we had never been there and were both totally convinced that it wouldn't be as picked over as the one in Manhattan. When we pulled into the parking lot and I saw all of these dumpy housewives in sweats, I practically started salivating. No competition. Inside, I went into a zone, filling a shopping cart to the brim with things like eight-dollar cashmere sweaters that had small holes in them, and I got into such an aroused state I was practically mowing people down with my cart. Then I got naked in the back of the store and frantically started trying on shit. I took such a long time that not only were we late for the wedding, we actually *missed* the ceremony.

Anyway, when I finally managed to corner Kat and ask her why she had all but abandoned the Church, which is a topic she likes to avoid, she looked me dead in the eye and said, it just wasn't fitting anymore. And she continued, when I started doing yoga all the time, I think it essentially replaced the good parts of church, and it also made me feel like my body was in prime condition and that I didn't have much time left to put it to good use.

I go, you stopped going to church and got into the most amazing shape you've ever been in your entire life because you wanted to start having sex? You're a total heretic.

And Kat goes, maybe.

Ever self-obsessed and thrilled with this turn of events, I say: Listen, it's thanks to me you're getting laid.

Kat goes: Maybe you did play a role in my demise. *Not* because I suddenly bought into all your arguments, but more because we had developed a really strong friendship. And it made me more confident and more willing to take risks and evaluate things. Look, P, be-coming friends with you was the catalyst—you didn't change the nature of the experiment, but maybe you sped the process along.

Me: How so?

Kat: It shakes things up when someone enters your life who you hold in such high esteem and who holds you in such high esteem.

Me: Who ever said I hold you in such high esteem?

Kat: You did.

Me: Oh. I guess I did. I do hold you in high esteem. You give me hope in humanity. I paused. Do you feel impure?

Kat: I do feel impure.

Me: Yeah, right.

Kat: I *do*.

Me: Believe me when I tell you that you're no more impure now than you were when you were a mission-ary in Geneva trying to turn people into fucking converts.

Kat: That's not true. When I was on my mission, I wasn't totally obsessed with myself. It felt healthy to not be consumed by totally vapid things all day. And I didn't buy new clothes for like a year and a half.

Me: Yeah, I've seen your photos—your outfits were absolutely repulsive. Plus, you don't have to be on a mission in order to not be totally obsessed with clothes, you know.

Kat: I'm working on it.

Me: What about the garments?

Kat: Oh, no. No, no, no.

This is the same thing she says *whenever* I ask her about the garments. Garments—contrary to the fact that they may sound like sexy lingerie—are *actually* a modern-day variant on the chastity belt. I mean, there's no hardware or anything, but for all intents and purposes, there may as well be. Or maybe there *should* be hardware on them, because even though Kat wore them for about five years, she still wound up in the bishop's office for engaging in sinful sexual behavior. Symbolically garments serve as a chastity belt, and most people who wear them take heed of that.

Married Mormon men and women are required to wear garments under their clothes. They get them at the temple (the temple recommend card comes into play here) either before going on a mission or before getting married. Whichever comes first, says Kat.

I found Kat's old garments when I was helping her

clean out her closet, and let me tell you, they're adorable. The top is this little cap-sleeved undershirt made of thin cuddly white cotton. I was like, I want these. I wish they came in camouflage.

She was like, *no way*, Periel. *No way*. And they do come in camouflage. You need to be in the military, though. *And* you need to present proof that you're in the military. And above and beyond that, as I've already explained to you, you need to present proof that you're a member in good standing with the Church.

I was like, *please. PLEASE!*

Nothing doing. She wasn't giving them up. I was like, Kat, be reasonable, you haven't worn these in years. They would keep me so warm in the winter.

Kat was like, Periel. There is no way I am giving you my garments.

I was like, Kat, you know my birthday is coming up.

Kat scrunched up her face the same way she did before she told Yonatan, I see us frolicking in a meadow. Then she said, no. I can't.

I was like, Kat, look, my intentions are very pure here. This isn't a joke to me. This is like a piece of art or something. I'm not trying to make a mockery of this, I *like* these things. I'm not going to tack them up on my wall and make some freak show out of them. You don't wear them, and I've taken a good deal of time to learn about them—

She goes, what do you mean?

I was like, well, for example, I know that those little markings all over the garments are there to remind you of your holy covenants.

Kat was very impressed with this.

So I continued. I've gone to church with you, I've been to fast and testimony, this isn't some novelty thing to me, I'm fucking interested.

I thought I was presenting a pretty strong case here.

I went on: I don't want you to do anything you don't want to do. I mean, I don't want them if you don't *want* to give them to me. (Pause.) So can I have them? You don't have to answer me right now, I want you to think about all this.

A few days later, I called her.

Me: So, what did you come up with?

Kat: Look, P. Even though you present a very compelling argument—*and* if I were to give my garments to anyone, it would be you—I can't do it. Even though I don't keep my temple covenants anymore, it would be, like, an act of hostility, you know? It would be like

I was dishonoring them. They're explicitly something you're not even supposed to show other people.

Me: So is your pussy. And you're doing that.

Kat: Well, not giving you the garments is a lot easier to hold true to. Plus, when you're talking about sex, there's a lot more in it for me.

Me: You're holding on by a thread, Kat.

Kat pouted. Maybe so.

Me: Actually, I take that back. You're not holding on by a thread. You're very grounded; you know exactly what's going on. You're the best Mormon I've ever met.

At this, she perked up. I am?

Me: Yes, you are. You're the best Mormon in the world. You're kind and generous and caring and you look out for people. It's a rare thing these days.

Kat looked at me.

I was like, I'm being serious, Kat. You're a real mensch.

Kat: A what?

Me: Kat, you're not going to ever be able to become a Jew if you don't know what a mensch is.

Kat: Who said I was becoming a Jew?

Me: You did. Back when you were fiddling around with Yonatan.

196

Kat: Oh yeah. Well, whatever. What's a mensch?

Me: It's a big compliment, believe me. It means you're, like, a decent human being. And like I said, there aren't so many of you left.

Kat goes, you're a mensch too, Periel. You're like my sister.

I go: You already have two sisters.

Kat goes: I know, but you don't.

Me: If I did, I'm sure I'd be much less of an ego-maniac. Or on second thought, maybe not, look at you.

Kat: You think I'm an egomaniac? I thought you just said I was a mensch.

Me: Well, you can be both. Look at me.

Kat: I am looking at you, and I already told you, you're like my sister. I would do anything for you.

Now it was my turn to perk up. I go, does that mean I can have your garments?

Kat scrunched up her face and started laughing. Then she said: Oh, Periel, come on.

about the author

Periel Aschenbrand identifies herself as half Israeli and half New York Jew. In addition to being a writer, she is founder and president of a politically oriented T-shirt company called body as billboard, which she hopes will continue to serve those who find it unappealing to be walking advertisements for corporate America. She lives in New York City. For more information go to www.bodyasbillboard.com.